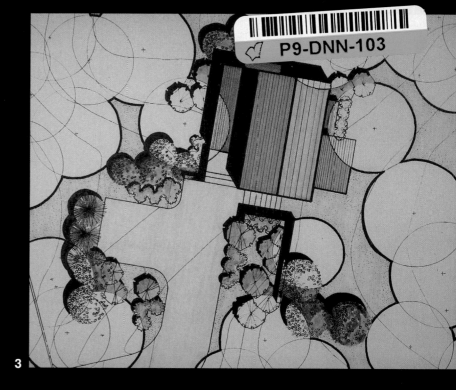

3

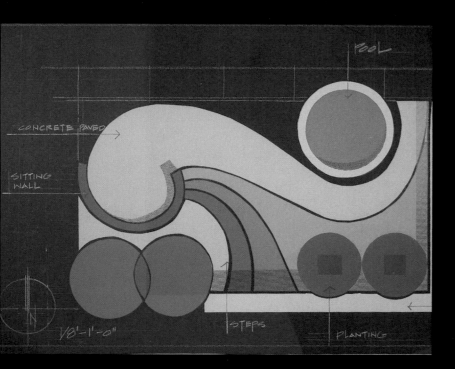

POOL

CONCRETE PAVED

SITTING
WALL

1/8"=1'-0"

STEPS

PLANTING

N

4

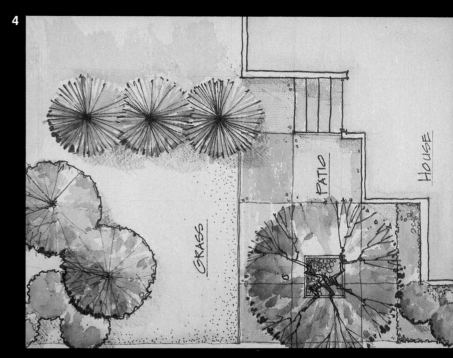

GRASS

PATIO

HOUSE

W. WASHINGTON ST.

SIDEWALK

TREE

DOWN

RAMP

STEP
UP

WALL

GROUND COVER

BENCH

SIDEWALK

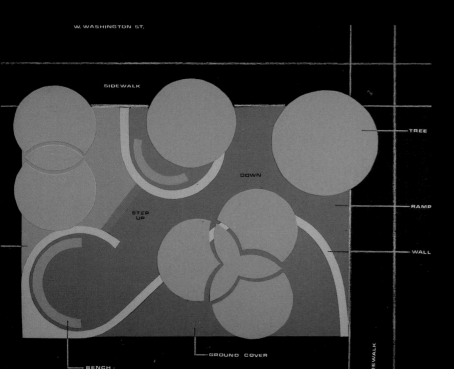

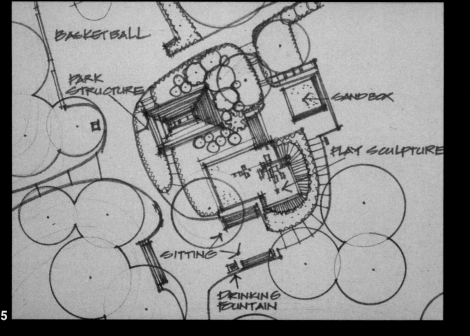

5

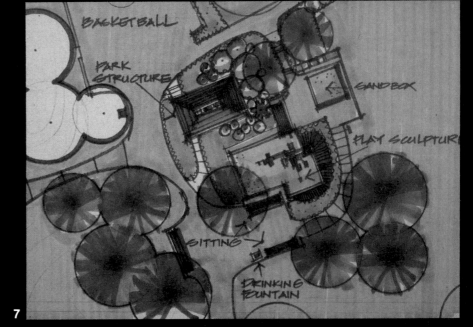

7

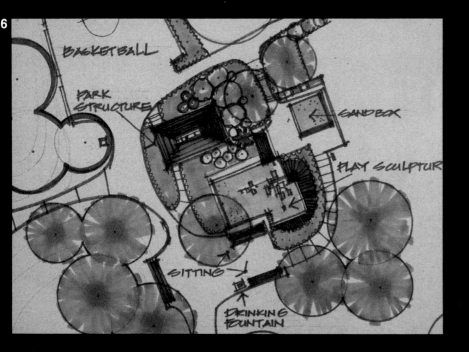

6

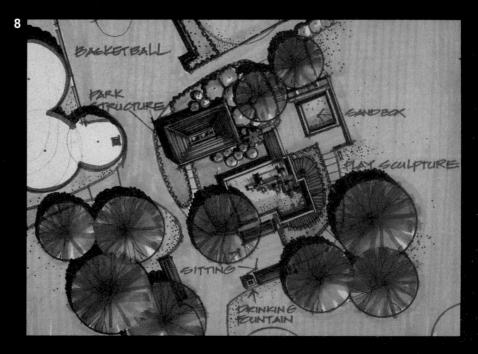

8

PLAN AND SECTION DRAWING

THOMAS C. WANG

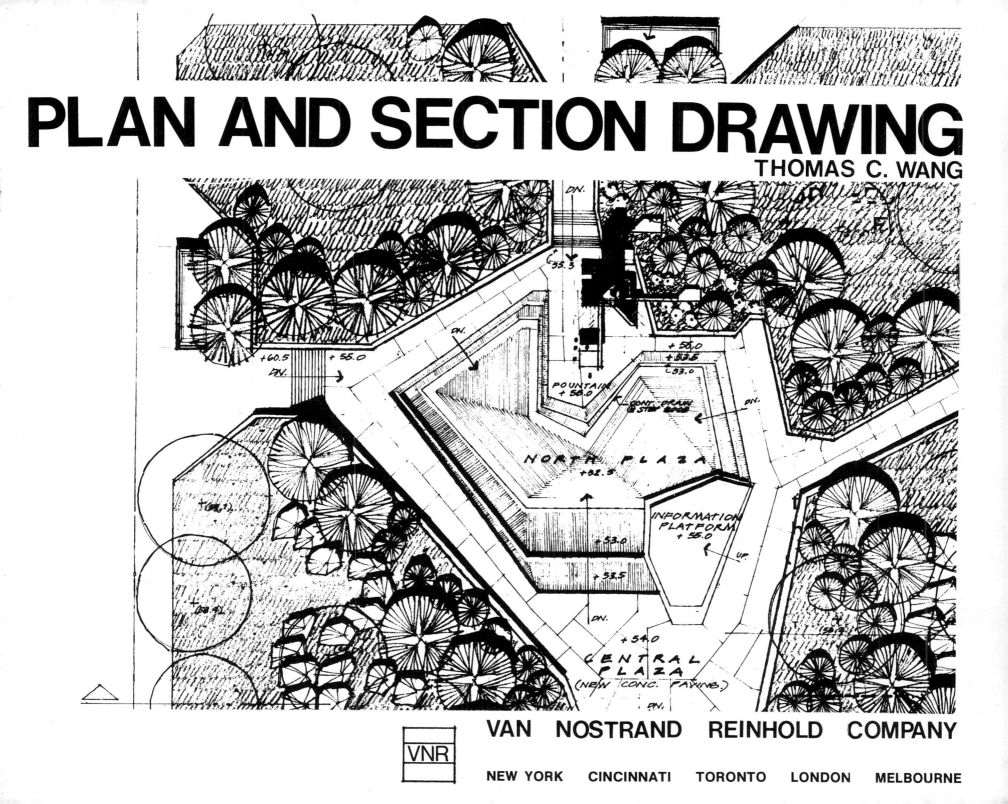

VAN NOSTRAND REINHOLD COMPANY

VNR

NEW YORK   CINCINNATI   TORONTO   LONDON   MELBOURNE

Copyright © 1979 by Litton Educational Publishing, Inc.
Library of Congress Catalog Card Number 78-12269
ISBN 0-442-26127-6 (cloth)
ISBN 0-442-29178-7 (paper)

Published in 1979 by Van Nostrand Reinhold Company
A division of Litton Educational Publishing, Inc.
135 West 50th Street, New York, N.Y. 10020, U.S.A.

Van Nostrand Reinhold Limited
1410 Birchmount Road, Scarborough, Ontario M1P 2E7, Canada

Van Nostrand Reinhold Australia Pty. Limited
17 Queen Street, Mitcham, Victoria 3132, Australia

Van Nostrand Reinhold Company Limited
Molly Millars Lane, Wokingham, Berkshire, England

16 15 14 13 12 11 10 9 8 7 6 5 4

Library of Congress Cataloging in Publication Data

Wang, Thomas C
  Plan and section drawing.

  Includes index.
  1. Architectural drawing—Technique. 2. Architectural
rendering—Technique. 3. Communication in architectural
design—Technique. I. Title.
NA2708.W36   720'.28   78-12269
ISBN 0-442-26127-6 (cloth)
ISBN 0-442-29178-7 (pbk)

Page 1: Student project, John Copley, University of Michigan.

Page 3: Johnson, Johnson, and Roy, Ann Arbor, Michigan.

Page 4: EDAW, Inc., Fort Collins, Colorado.

Color Plate 1: Color-Aids on black illustration board, class demonstration.

Color Plate 2: Color-Aids on black illustration board, student project (Richard Smeltzer, University of Michigan).

Color Plate 3: Markers on blackline print, student project (Patricia Graham, University of Illinois).

Color Plate 4: Watercolor on Strathmore paper, class demonstration.

Color Plates 5—8: Step-by-step illustration of marker application on brownline print; color pencils used for highlighting.

Color Plate 9: Pentel markers on yellow tracing paper.

Color Plate 10: Markers on brownline print (light background).

Color Plate 11: Markers on brownline print (dark background).

Color Plate 12: Watercolor on Strathmore paper.

Color Plates 13—14: Marker and color pencil brownline print, class demonstration.

Color Plates 15—16: Marker on brownline print, Mitchell Associates Inc., Portland, Oregon.

Pages 13-16: Johnson, Johnson and Roy, Ann Arbor, Michigan.

Pages 17-21: Johnson, Johnson and Roy, Ann Arbor, Michigan.

Page 27: EDAW Inc., Fort Collins, Colorado.

Page 34: Student project, Sara Liss, University of Michigan.

Page 40: Johnson, Johnson and Roy, Ann Arbor, Michigan.

Pages 43, 46, 50: Student project, John Copley, University of Michigan.

Page 53: EDAW, Inc., Fort Collins, Colorado (left); Johnson, Johnson and Roy, Ann Arbor, Michigan (right).

Page 55: Mitchell Associates Inc., Portland, Oregon.

Page 58: EDAW Inc., Fort Collins, Colorado.

Pages 77-79: Mitchell Associates Inc., Portland, Oregon.

Page 80: Student project, John Copley, University of Michigan.

Page 81: Johnson, Johnson and Roy, Ann Arbor, Michigan.

Page 82: Student project, Sara Liss, University of Michigan.

Page 83: Student project, John Copley, University of Michigan.

Pages 84-86: Johnson, Johnson and Roy, Ann Arbor, Michigan.

Page 87: Mitchell Associates Inc., Portland, Oregon.

Page 88: EDAW Inc., Fort Collins, Colorado.

Page 89: Mitchell Associates Inc., Portland, Oregon.

Pages 90-94: Student project, John Copley, University of Michigan.

Page 95: EDAW Inc., Fort Collins, Colorado.

to my wife Jacqueline

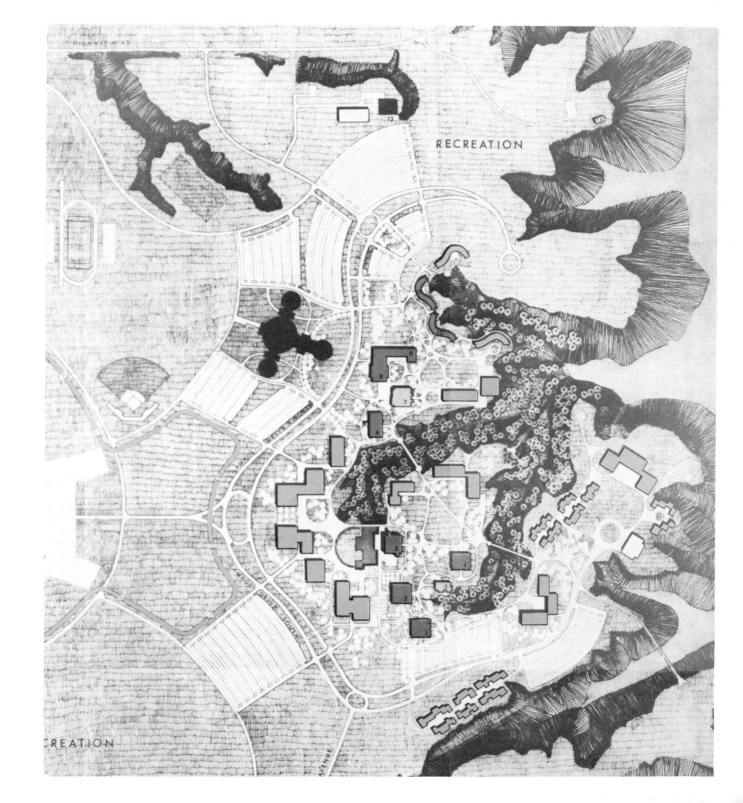

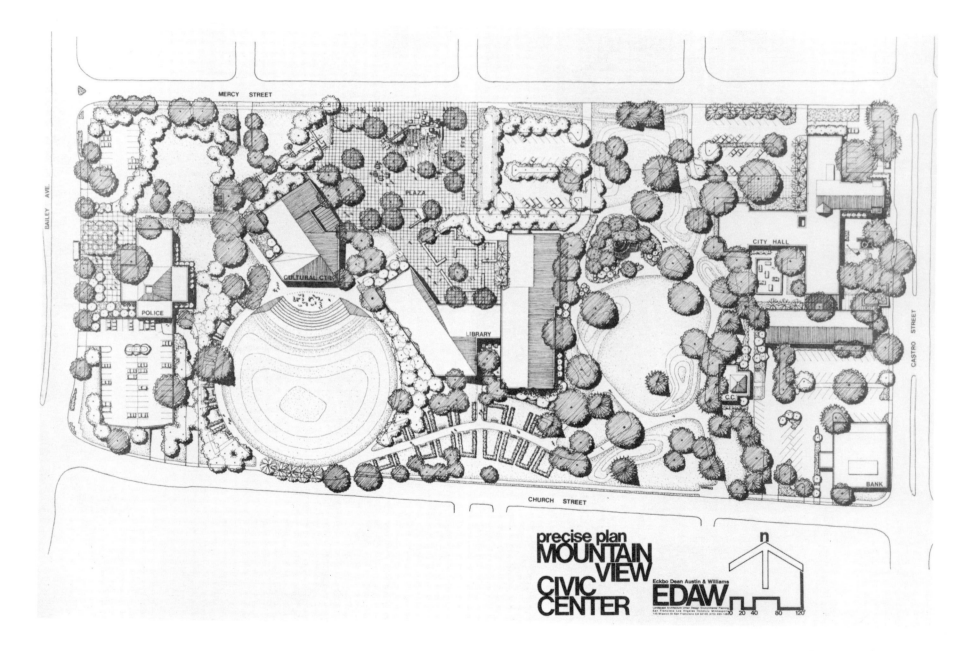

MERCY STREET

BAILEY AVE.

PLAZA

CULTURAL CTR.

POLICE

LIBRARY

CITY HALL

CASTRO STREET

C.C.

BANK

CHURCH STREET

precise plan
MOUNTAIN
VIEW
CIVIC
CENTER

Eckbo Dean Austin & Williams
EDAW

n

20 40   80   120

Table of Contents

	Foreword	6
Chapter 1:	Introduction	7
Chapter 2:	Line	22
Chapter 3:	Buildings	27
Chapter 4:	Trees	34
Chapter 5:	Shrubs	41
Chapter 6:	Ground Covers	44
Chapter 7:	Overlappings and Shadows	47
Chapter 8:	Pavements	50
Chapter 9:	Water	52
Chapter 10:	Cars	54
Chapter 11:	Roads	56
Chapter 12:	Sections and Elevations	59
Chapter 13:	Line Weight and Vertical Exaggeration	64
Chapter 14:	Plant Materials	68
Chapter 15:	Shadows	76
Chapter 16:	Examples	77
	Index	96

Foreword

Plan and section are drawings that communicate design ideas. These drawings record and assist in the evolution of design processes and pictorialize the images of the final products. They also illustrate the methods of construction and are part of the legal documentation when the projects are built. Above all, plan and section are not simply attractive pictures prepared solely for the purpose of showing the clients and others how the finished product will look. They come in different formats that represent different stages of the design development. They must carry specific messages to the viewers. The symbols used in these drawings should be recognizable to prevent misinterpretation. Dimensioning and scale should be precise and clearly labeled.

The teaching of plan and section drawing is very important in design education. The techniques taught tend to reflect different individual methods and are not well documented. It is therefore my intent to discuss the various aspects of plan and section drawing separately and to illustrate the fundamental principles in simple terms. This book is not intended to be a graphic reference but rather to emphasize the "how to" aspect of drawing, and I hope it will be a helpful guide to those who are beginning to communicate graphically.

aerial photograph

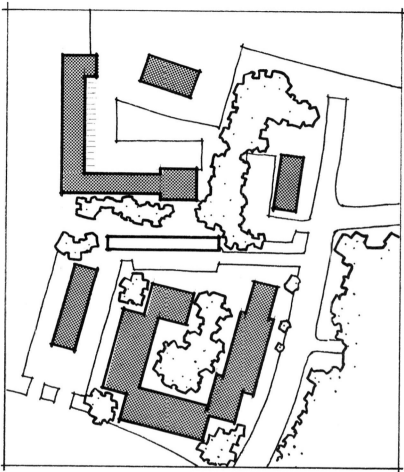

a site plan

Plan drawing is a kind of orthographic projection. It is very similar to aerial photographs, which not only show the horizontal distance between objects but also identify them.

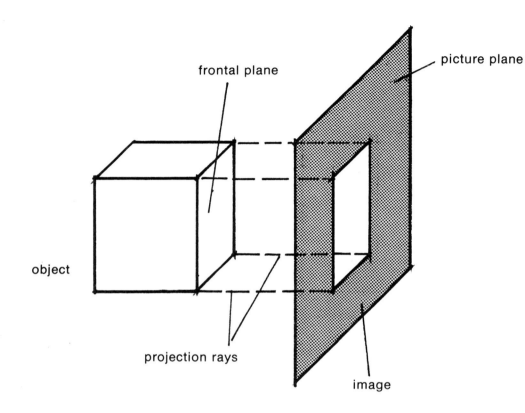

frontal plane

picture plane

object

projection rays

image

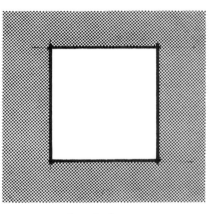

front view

In orthographic projection the picture plane intercepts parallel projection rays from the frontal plane of the object. The projection rays are always perpendicular to the picture plane.

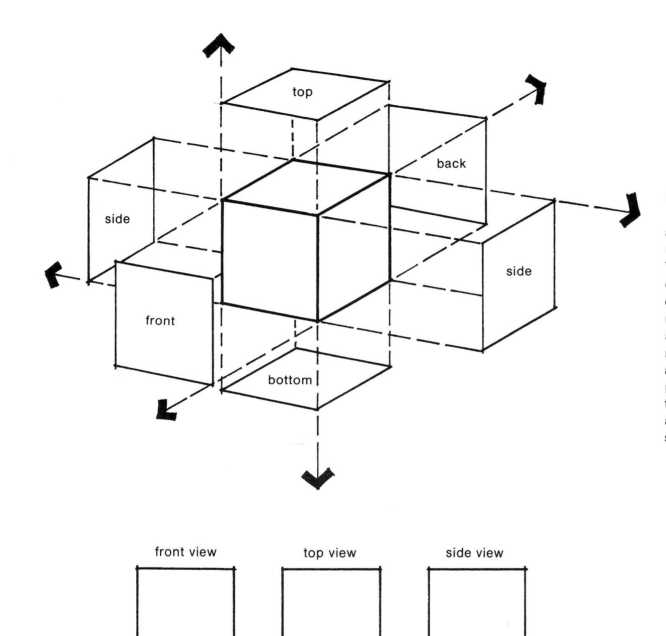

top

back

side

side

front

bottom

Every rectangular object has six sides (views). In order to understand the shape of the object and the adjacent relationships between planes, multiview projection is used to describe it. Three views (top, front, and side) are the most common projections used to describe the object graphically. Multiview projection is most often used in product design, in which accurate measurement and exact image representation are required. In architecture and landscape-architecture design multiview projection is frequently used under different terminologies. A top view is the same as a plan, and section and elevation are equivalent to a side view.

front view   top view   side view

9

topographic map

building plan

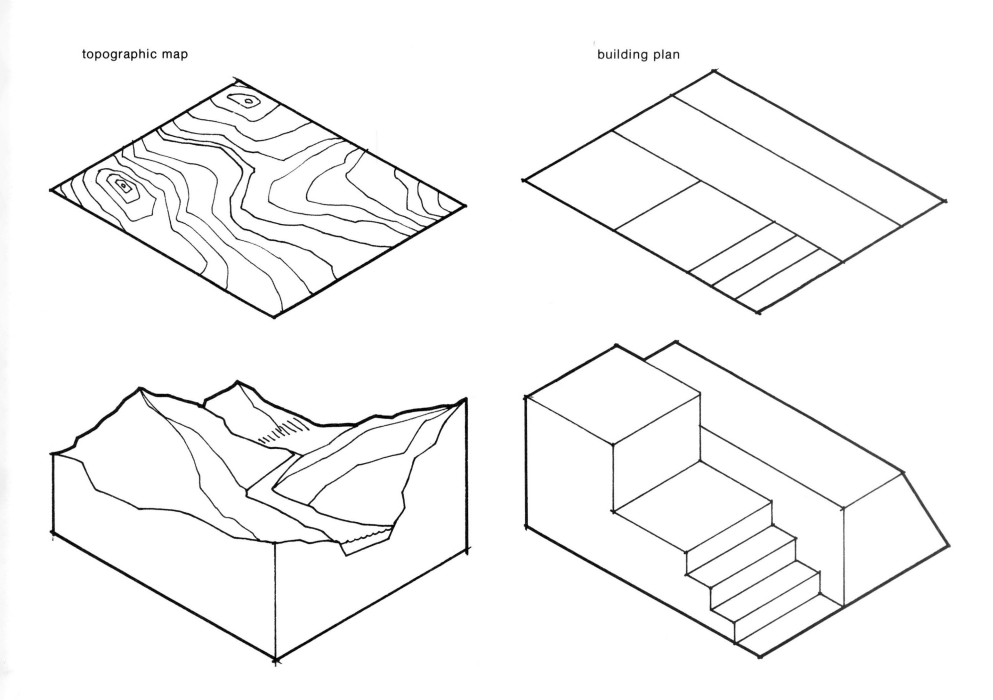

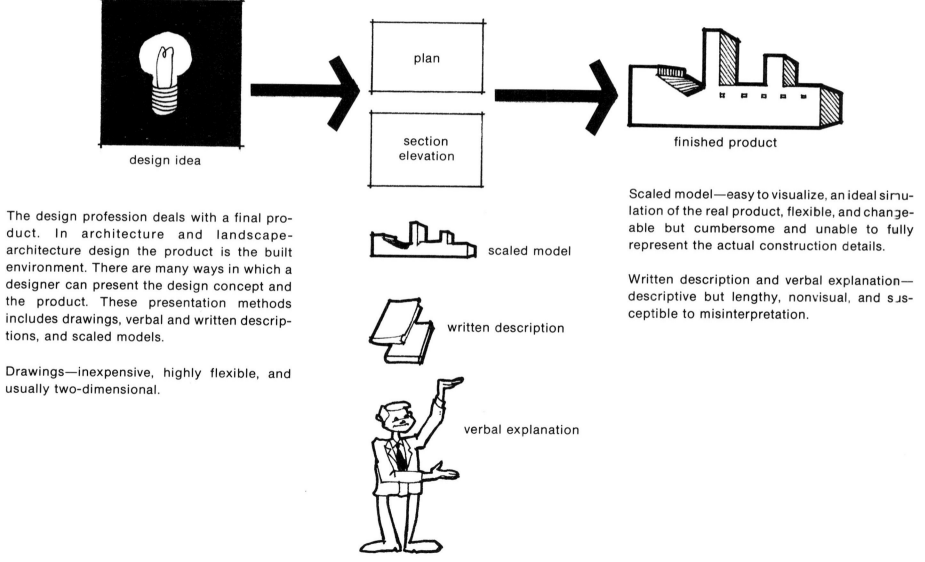

design idea

plan

section
elevation

finished product

scaled model

written description

verbal explanation

The design profession deals with a final product. In architecture and landscape-architecture design the product is the built environment. There are many ways in which a designer can present the design concept and the product. These presentation methods includes drawings, verbal and written descriptions, and scaled models.

Drawings—inexpensive, highly flexible, and usually two-dimensional.

Scaled model—easy to visualize, an ideal simulation of the real product, flexible, and changeable but cumbersome and unable to fully represent the actual construction details.

Written description and verbal explanation—descriptive but lengthy, nonvisual, and susceptible to misinterpretation.

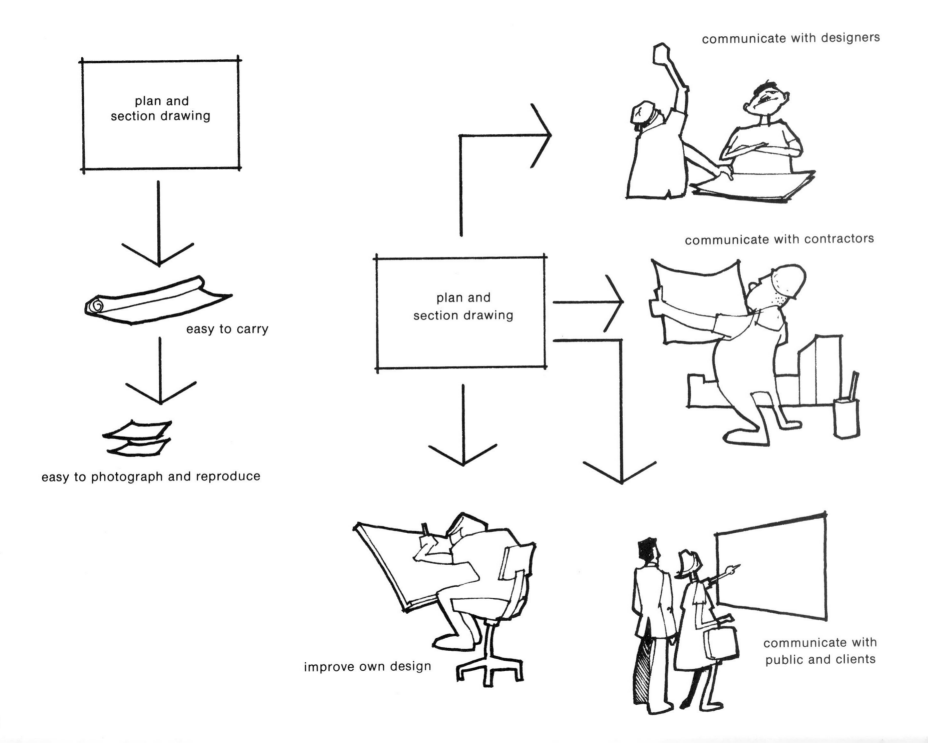

communicate with designers

plan and
section drawing

easy to carry

easy to photograph and reproduce

plan and
section drawing

communicate with contractors

improve own design

communicate with
public and clients

There are many different types of plan drawing, and each has its own purpose. The following illustrations demonstrate the use of different types of plan drawings in a complete design process.

Regional map—a map that shows the entire region. It covers up to a 15-mile radius from the study center.

Vicinity map—a map that shows the adjacent land uses that surround the study area. It usually covers the same watershed or township or is bounded by the major road system.

regional map

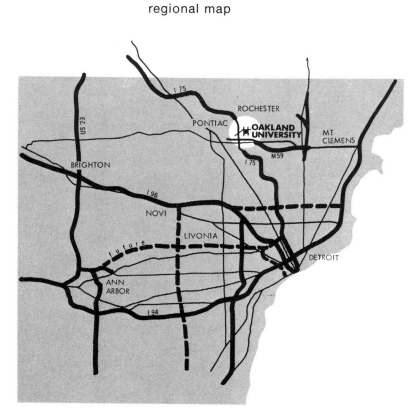

vicinity map

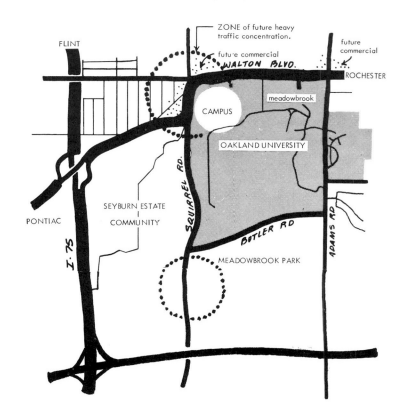

Site-information Maps

These are maps that contain necessary background information about the site. This data is often available from sources such as the Soil Survey or Public Works Department. Data maps frequently used by environmental designers are the soil map, the land-use map, and the vegetation map.

site-survey map

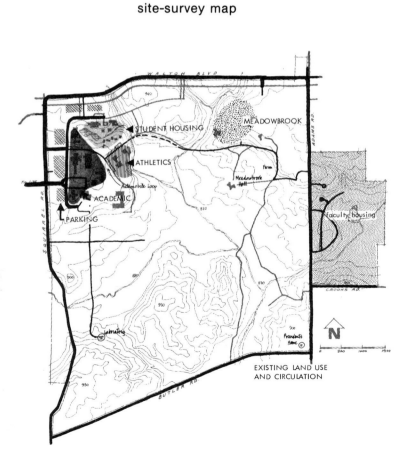

EXISTING LAND USE
AND CIRCULATION

site-analysis map

BUILDABLE LAND AREAS

- wet sands, silts
- peat muck
- major tree cover
- prime development plateaus

conceptual diagrams

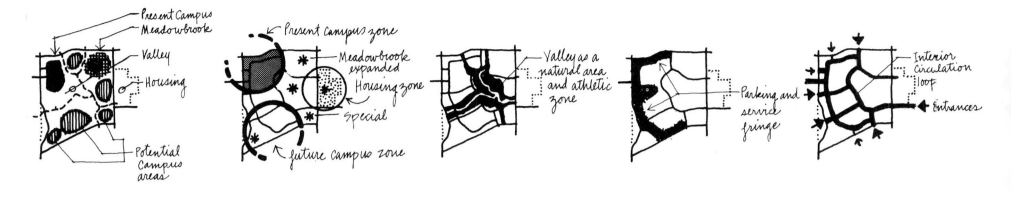

Present Campus
Meadowbrook
Valley
Housing
Potential Campus areas

Present campus zone
Meadowbrook expanded
Housing zone
Special
future campus zone

Valley as a natural area and athletic zone

Parking and service fringe

Interior Circulation loop
Entrances

conceptual layout maps

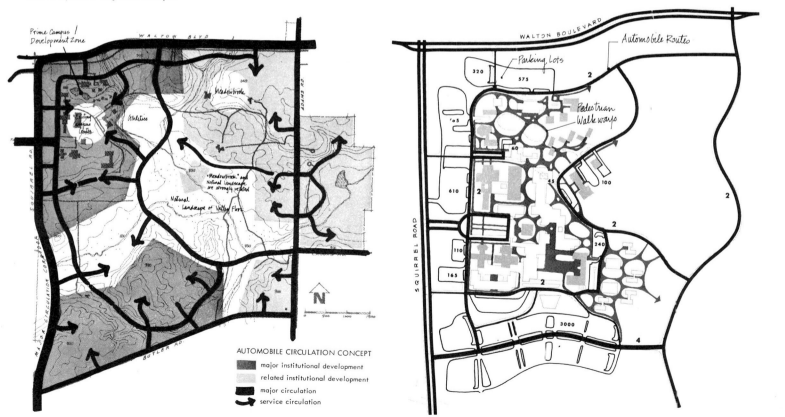

Prime Campus / Development Zone

WALTON BLVD
Meadowbrook
Athletics
Existing Campus Center

"Meadowbrook" and Natural landscape are strongly related

Natural Landscape of Valley Floor

ADAMS RD.

SQUIRREL RD.

MAJOR CIRCULATION CORRIDOR

BUTLER RD.

N

AUTOMOBILE CIRCULATION CONCEPT
■ major institutional development
□ related institutional development
■ major circulation
➤ service circulation

WALTON BOULEVARD
Automobile Routes
Parking Lots
Pedestrian Walkways

SQUIRREL ROAD

320
575
'05
60
610
45
100
110
165
240
2
2
2
2
2
2
3000
4

master plan and perspective

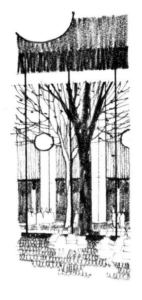

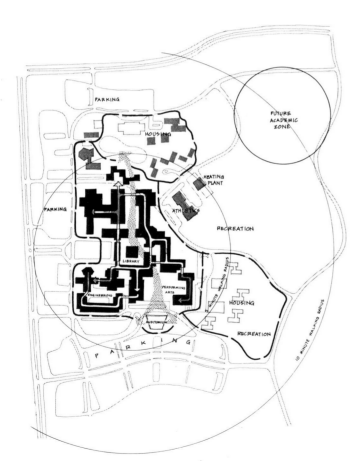

Bubble Diagrams

These diagrammatic drawings are very important in concept development during the design process. They are the graphic shorthand that records the designer's thought process and the ideas that are generated. These diagrams are highly abstract and symbolic. Written descriptions are needed to help others to understand.

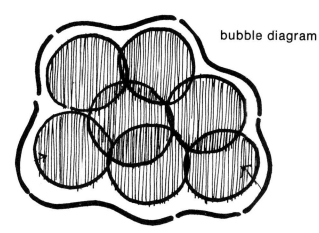

bubble diagram

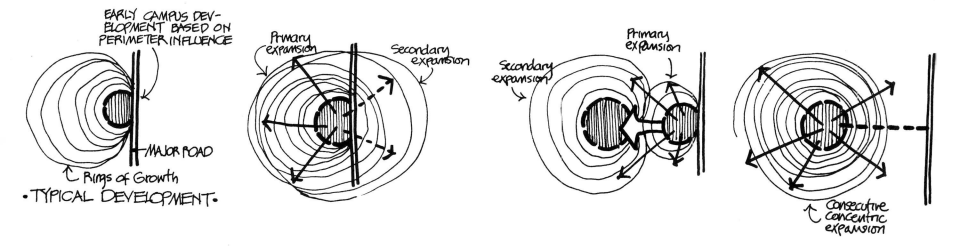

evolution of bubble diagram

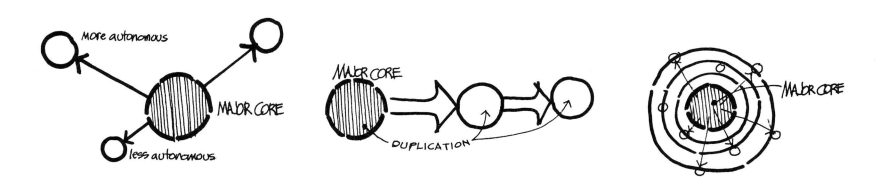

Conceptual Diagrams

These diagrams are derived directly from bubble diagrams. They are highly abstract and symbolic.

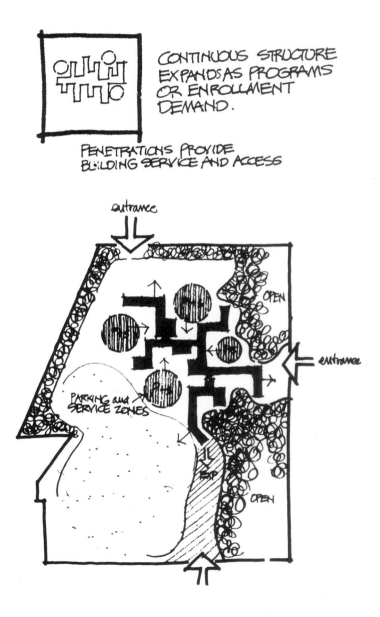

CONTINUOUS STRUCTURE EXPANDS AS PROGRAMS OR ENROLLMENT DEMAND.

PENETRATIONS PROVIDE BUILDING SERVICE AND ACCESS

Conceptual Maps

In these maps the refined concept is drawn on top of the base map. Concepts can therefore be site-specific.

Site-analysis Maps

These maps record the results of site analysis. This is a rather subjective process of interpretation based on the concepts and objectives of the design project.

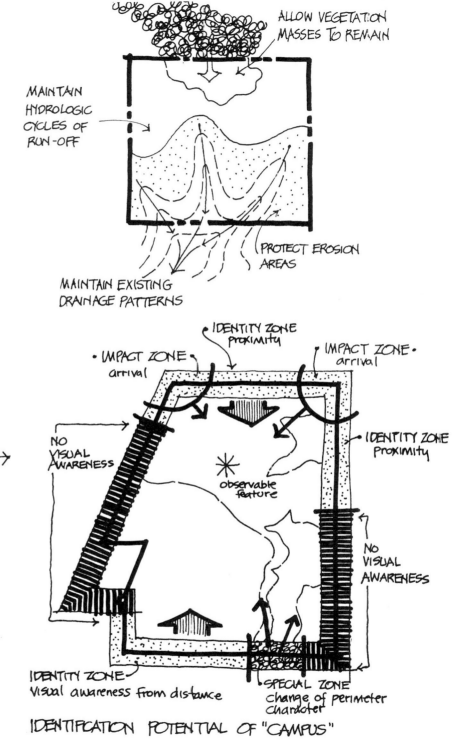

ALLOW VEGETATION MASSES TO REMAIN

MAINTAIN HYDROLOGIC CYCLES OF RUN-OFF

PROTECT EROSION AREAS

MAINTAIN EXISTING DRAINAGE PATTERNS

IMPACT ZONE arrival

IDENTITY ZONE proximity

IMPACT ZONE arrival

NO VISUAL AWARENESS

observable feature

IDENTITY ZONE proximity

NO VISUAL AWARENESS

IDENTITY ZONE visual awareness from distance

SPECIAL ZONE change of perimeter character

IDENTIFICATION POTENTIAL OF "CAMPUS"

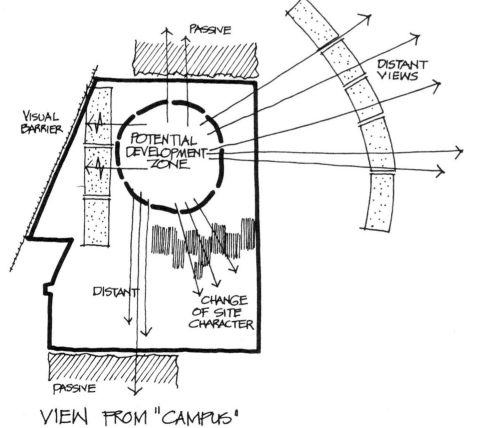

PASSIVE

DISTANT VIEWS

VISUAL BARRIER

POTENTIAL DEVELOPMENT ZONE

DISTANT

CHANGE OF SITE CHARACTER

PASSIVE

VIEW FROM "CAMPUS"

Preliminary-design Maps

The following four examples illustrate the birth of a design solution. It evolved on different layers of tracing paper. Design ideas are recorded on tracing paper, and design concepts and objectives are tested and compared. A solution is eventually evolved and finalized that satisfies most of the requirements.

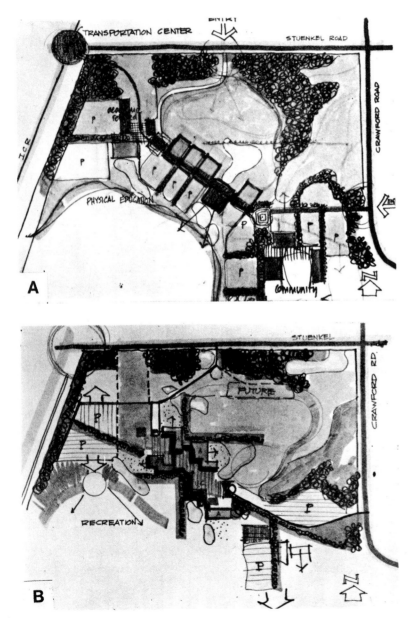

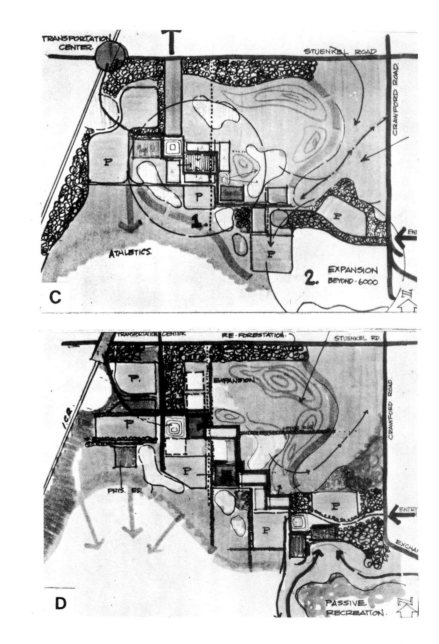

Final Site-development Plan

This is also called the master plan. It shows the final design solution and includes building masses, road layouts, planting schemes, and the location of all design elements. Depending on the nature of the design project, the format of the master plan varies from a detailed precise document to a general schematic layout.

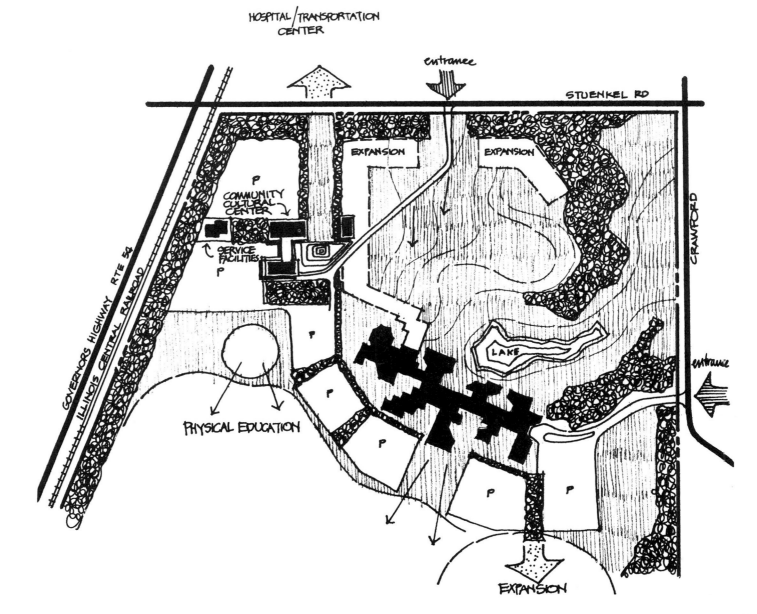

2 Line

line o—————————————————————o

------------------------------ dotted line

— — — — — — — — — — short dashed line

—— —— —— —— —— —— long dashed line

——— ——— ——— ——— extra long dashed line

————————————————— continuous line

The basic symbol for all drawings is line. Line defines spatial edges, renders volume, creates textures, and connects to form alphabets and numbers. Linework in plan and section drawings should be sharp and dense, with uniform width and consistent value. There are five basic line types: dotted, short-dash, long-dash, extralong-dash, and continuous.

Dotted lines represent unseen edges of objects. Continuous lines represent visible edges of objects.

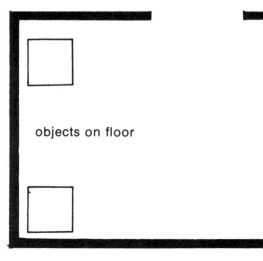

objects on floor

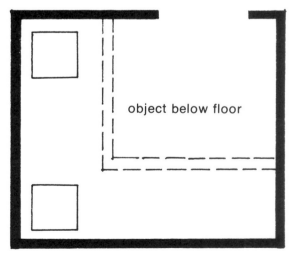

object below floor

Short-dash or dotted lines represent hidden or unseen objects in front of or below the observer. They also point out future construction items that are not included within the contract limit.

Long-dash lines represent hidden or unseen items behind or above the observer. They also indicate items within the construction limit that are to be removed.

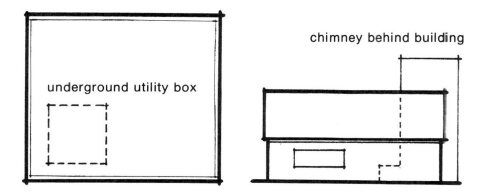

underground utility box

chimney behind building

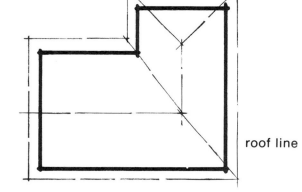

roof line

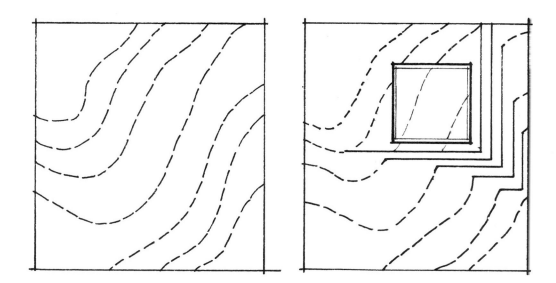

Contour lines before grading are usually shown by long-dash lines. Finished grades are shown by continuous lines.

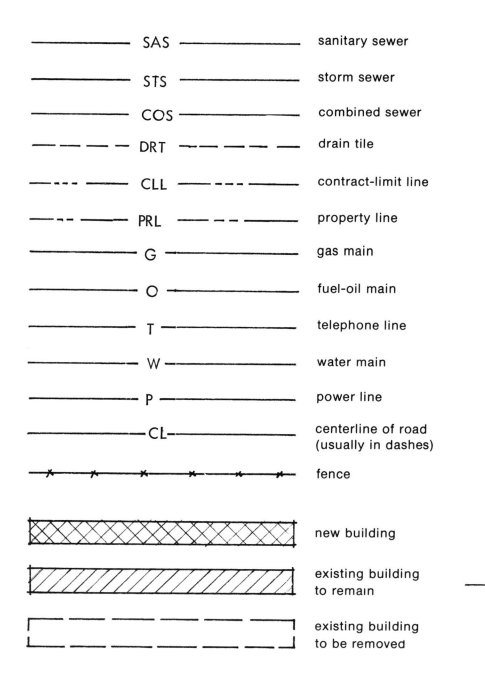

SAS	sanitary sewer
STS	storm sewer
COS	combined sewer
DRT	drain tile
CLL	contract-limit line
PRL	property line
G	gas main
O	fuel-oil main
T	telephone line
W	water main
P	power line
CL	centerline of road (usually in dashes)
✕ fence	fence
new building	new building
existing building to remain	existing building to remain
existing building to be removed	existing building to be removed

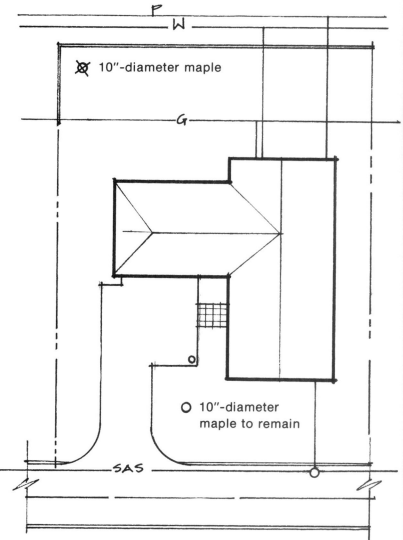

10"-diameter maple

10"-diameter maple to remain

There are five basic line widths: extrathick, thick, medium, thin, and extrathin. There are no standardized measurements for each width. The widths of lines are relative and depend mostly on the overall size of the drawing. Thin lines may be quite appropriate for a small drawing but may be almost invisible in a large plan.

Extrathick lines—for large-size drawing-sheet borders, title-block borders, and specific graphic symbols that require accentuation.

Thick lines—for mass profiles, tree masses, building edges (walls and partitions), and selected title-block borders.

Medium lines—for smaller-scale mass profiles, design elements, and interior layouts.

Thin lines—for design elements, internal profiles, partition lines (brick patterns), and dimensioning in a working drawing.

Extrathin lines—for lettering guides, layouts, texturing, and dimensioning.

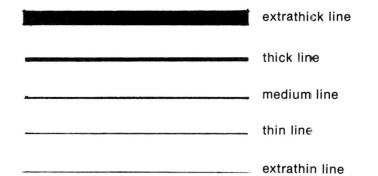

extrathick line

thick line

medium line

thin line

extrathin line

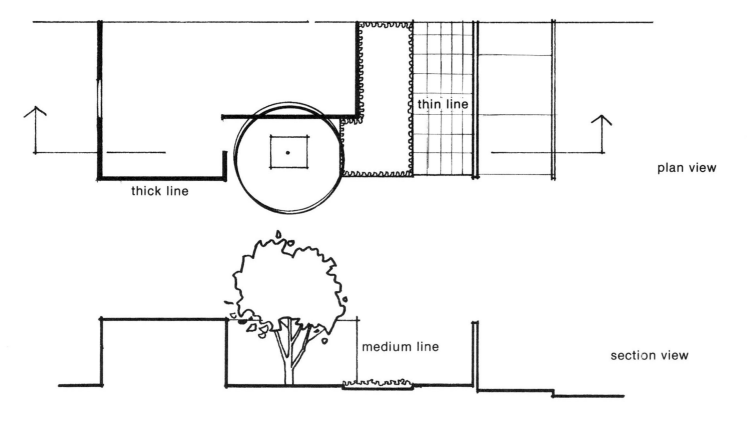

thin line

thick line

plan view

medium line

section view

In a working drawing profile lines of construction details should be drawn with a thick line. Use thin or extrathin lines for texturing the materials. Dimension lines should be thin, with a heavy, short dash at the dimension-line intersection.

In a section or elevation drawing profile lines of the ground should be drawn with a relatively thick line. Edges of trees should be connected with a medium line. Objects at a distance should be outlined with a thin line.

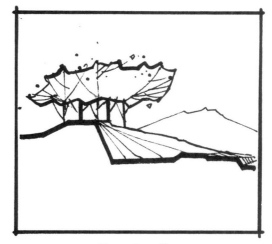

section elevation

4" HOLE

construction detail

In a plan view a building edge (wall) should be drawn with a thick line. Design elements (benches, plantings) should be rendered with a medium line. Edges of trees should be gone over with a thick border. Use a thin line for patterns and textures.

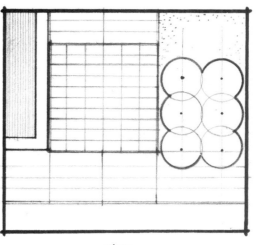

plan

Buildings 3

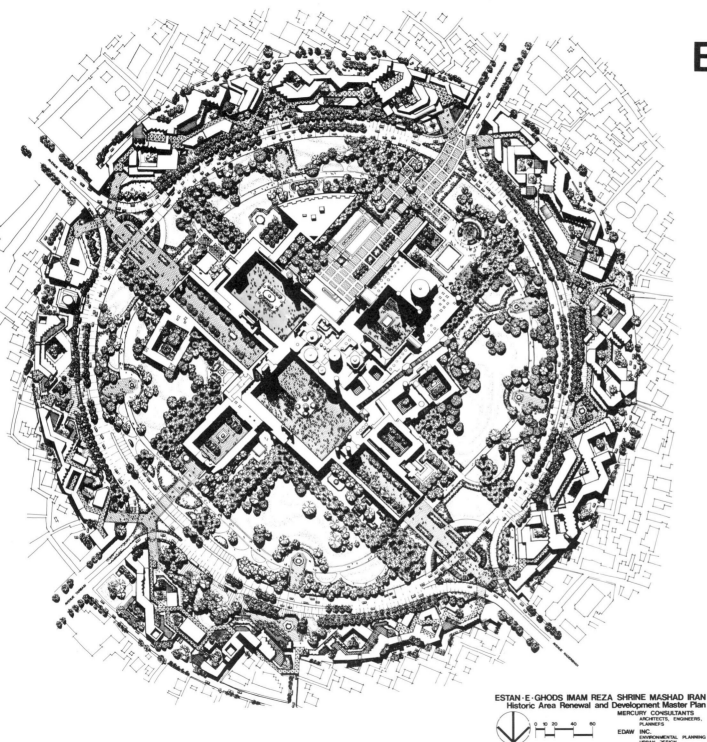

Buildings and plant materials are the two most frequently used symbols in plan drawing. They are the major components of the built environment that the designers are responsible for creating. Drawings of buildings should respond to different eras and their respective styles. Modern buildings are more massive but simple in appearance. Older buildings are more elaborate in detail. The plan drawing looks at buildings from the top. It emphasizes the horizontal dimension of the structure, and edges are therefore the most important feature. Edges of buildings should be bold, sharp, and accurately drawn.

ESTAN·E·GHODS IMAM REZA SHRINE MASHAD IRAN
Historic Area Renewal and Development Master Plan

MERCURY CONSULTANTS
ARCHITECTS, ENGINEERS, PLANNERS

EDAW INC.
ENVIRONMENTAL PLANNING
URBAN DESIGN
LANDSCAPE ARCHITECTURE

0 10 20 40 60

NORTH

27

A thin line drawing has weak spatial edges. They should be differentiated from the rest of the lines representing other design elements.

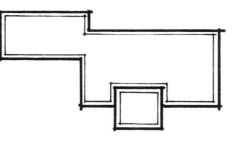

Buildings are unique geometric forms. A top view of the building with a flat top is usually not very attractive. The utility box and stair tower are interesting features that give the rooftop a more sculptural look.

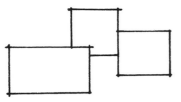

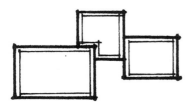

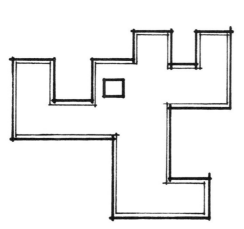

A thick profile line with a thin line inside. This double line begins to define a stronger edge and gives the building a more massive appearance.

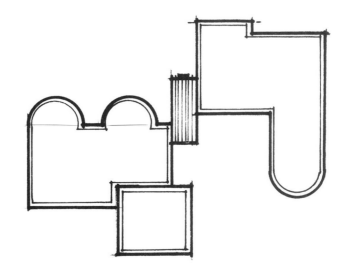

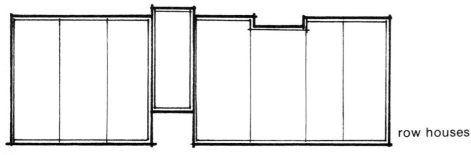

row houses

Use curvilinear lines to break up the monotony of the rectangular outline.

28

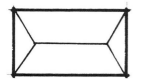

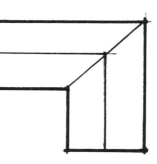

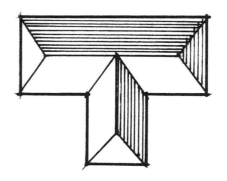

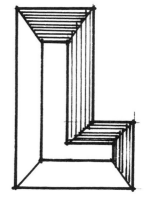

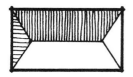

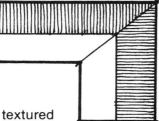

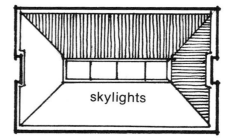

A building with a pitch roof should be textured to increase the three-dimensional quality. Roofs without texture tend to have a flat appearance.

skylights

In texturing a roof begin to bring out the feeling of depth. It gives the viewer a better understanding of the roof form.

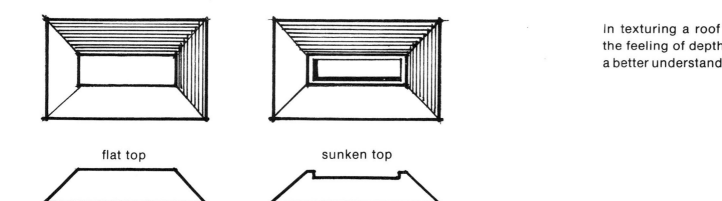

flat top

sunken top

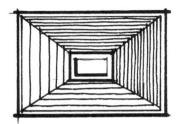

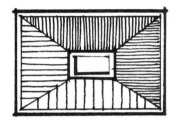

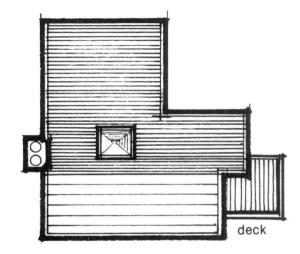

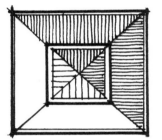

deck

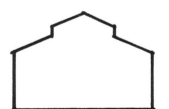

enclosed court

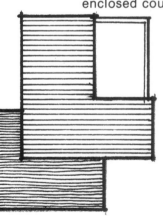

The shaded side of the roof should have a denser texture than the sun side. These textures can also be used to represent the roofing materials and the direction in which they were laid.

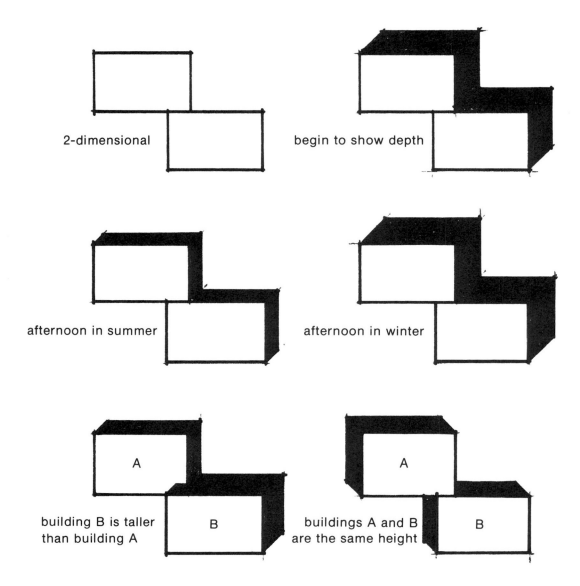

2-dimensional

begin to show depth

afternoon in summer

afternoon in winter

building B is taller
than building A

buildings A and B
are the same height

Shadow brings out the three-dimensional quality of the drawing. It depicts the heights of objects, differentiates times, and indicates the surface condition of the ground.

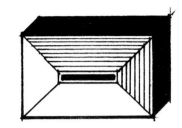

Shadow in a plan drawing is merely a symbol. It doesn't have to be accurately measured according to the bearing and altitude of the sun. A realistic shadow pattern is usually too long and might cover up most of the interesting design details on the ground plane.

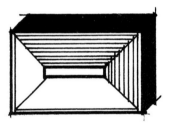
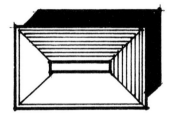

recessed shadow indicates extension of roof overhang

The angle of the shadow should be consistent. The length of the shadow should be the same for buildings with the same height.

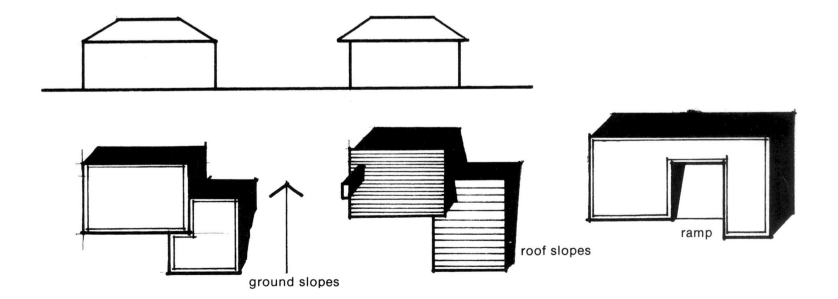

ground slopes

roof slopes

ramp

shadow up

A more realistic shadow for the Northern Hemisphere.

shadow down

Some artists think that the shadow reads better when it is pointing down.

solid black

For a short shadow, this design provides maximum contrast and opacity.

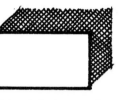

cross-hatching

This style has a nice semi-transparent texture, but takes time to draw.

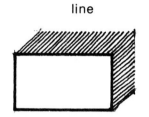

line

This has good texture but is easily confused with other lines on the ground plane (especially pavements).

Zip-a-tone

This saves time and is easy to use but is incompatible with a hand-drawn plan.

avoid   OK   good

4 Trees

Plant material is probably the most important symbol in landscape-architecture drawing. It plays a important role in design because it creates space, defines spatial edges, adds colors to the environment, and provides shade. Tree symbols enhance the plan drawing.

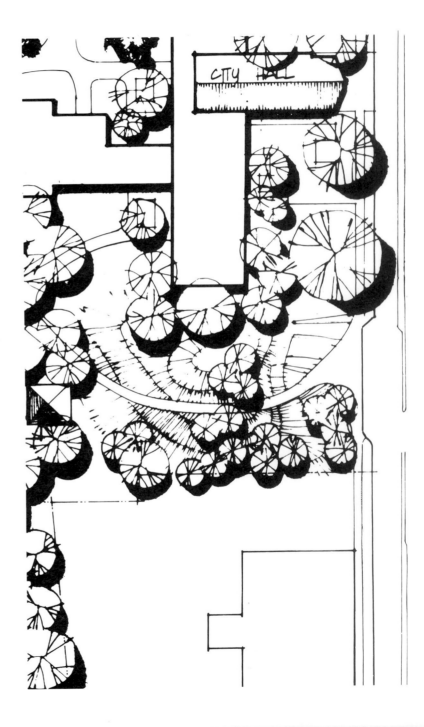

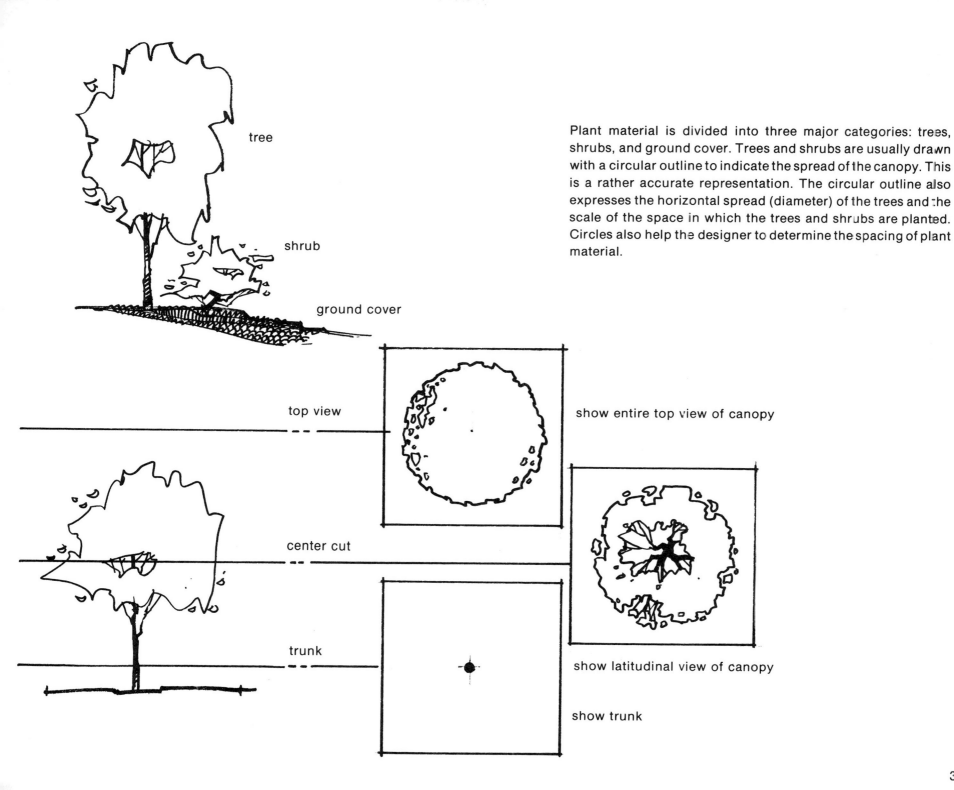

tree

shrub

ground cover

Plant material is divided into three major categories: trees, shrubs, and ground cover. Trees and shrubs are usually drawn with a circular outline to indicate the spread of the canopy. This is a rather accurate representation. The circular outline also expresses the horizontal spread (diameter) of the trees and the scale of the space in which the trees and shrubs are planted. Circles also help the designer to determine the spacing of plant material.

top view — show entire top view of canopy

center cut — show latitudinal view of canopy

trunk — show trunk

 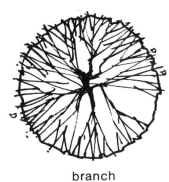

branch

texture

outline

There are three basic ways to draw trees in plan: branch, out-line, and texture. Outline has a solid, opaque appearance. Plant materials and other design elements are usually not shown underneath this kind of symbol. Branch and texture are more realistic. The silhouette effect of these styles allows the viewer to see through the canopy.

deciduous trees

evergreen trees

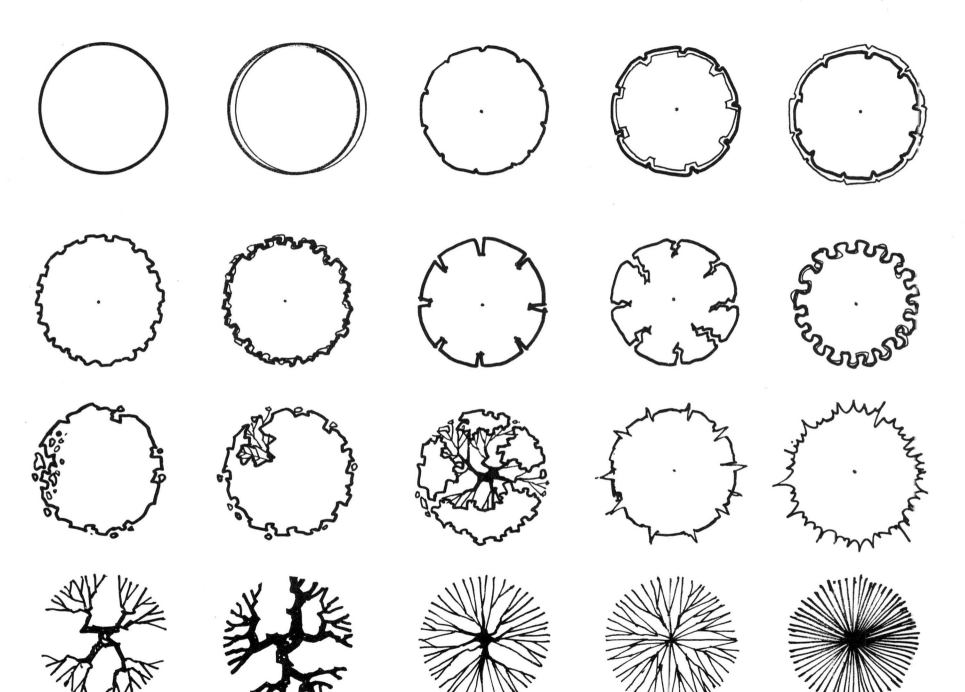

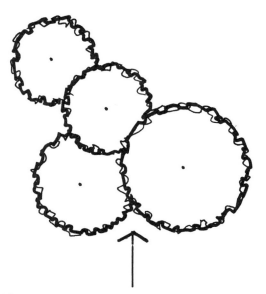

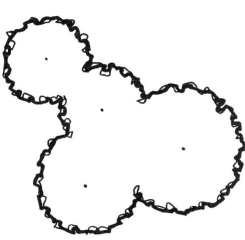

The major function of plant material is to make space. Trees are often shown in groups to create a more defined edge.

Overlapping should be carefully avoided. Outline the tree edge with a thick line. Use a thin pencil line to define individual trees.

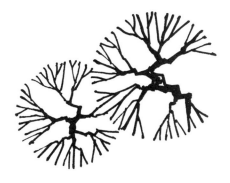

Avoid overlapping branch and texture symbols. Larger trees are always shown above smaller ones. Branches and textures should be carefully spaced to prevent excessive complexity when symbols overlap.

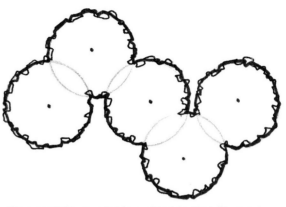

Plot the tree with a thin pencil outline. Use a circle template.

Select the appropriate symbol. Outline the circumference with a thick line.

For certain symbols a double line is used to obtain a better-defined edge. It increases the massiveness of trees.

Draw a circle with the aid of a circle template.

Outline the major branches with a soft pencil.

Fill in the complete branching pattern. Don't go over the edge of the circle.

sketchy trees

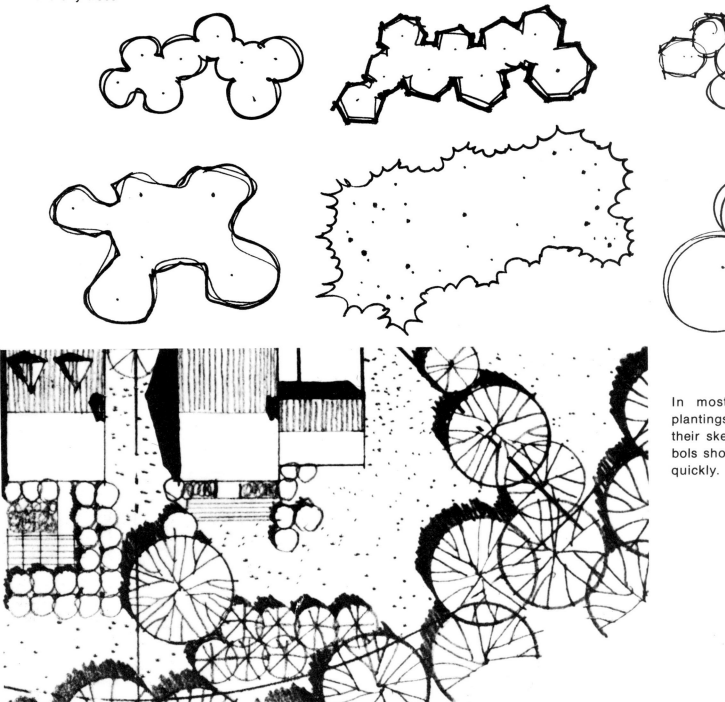

In most preliminary-design plans plantings are drawn freehand. Despite their sketchy appearance these symbols should be drawn accurately and quickly.

In plan drawings shrubs are the same as trees: the same
symbol can be used for both. The key determining factor is
the scale of the drawing.

Shrubs 5

plan view

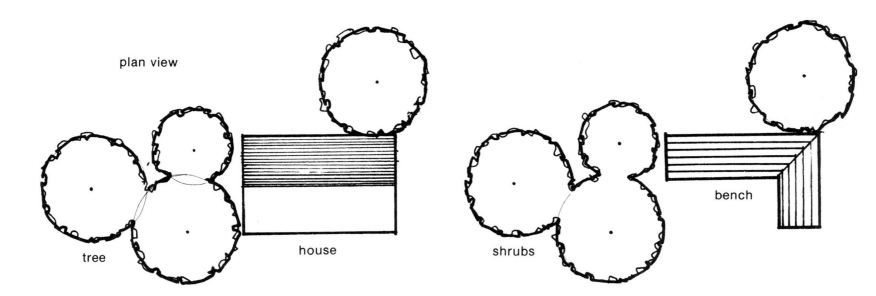

tree   house   shrubs   bench

elevation

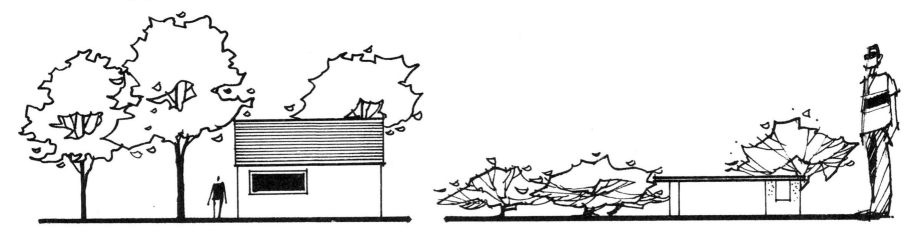

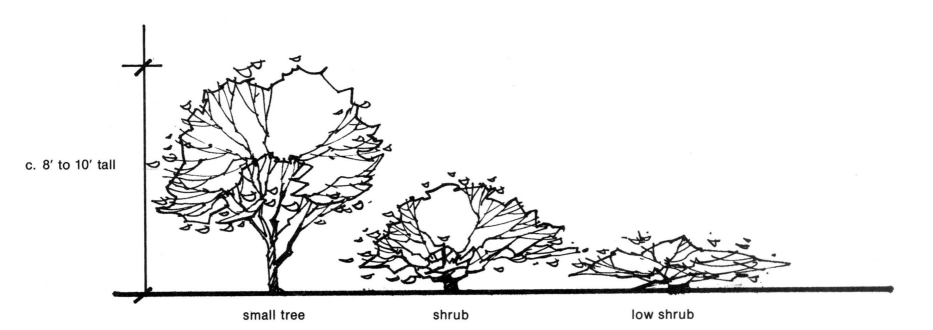

c. 8' to 10' tall

| small tree | shrub | low shrub |

shrubs are usually planted in groups

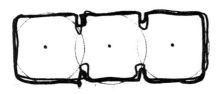

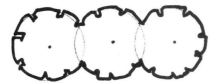
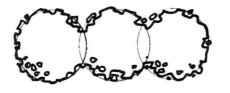
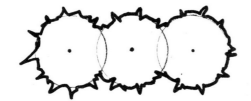

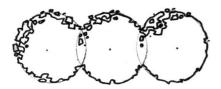
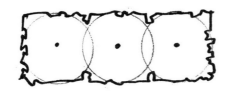

Outline symbols are more appropriate for small shrubs because of their massive and solid look. Texture and branch symbols are too busy and complex for the smaller shrubs. They are especially inappropriate when shrubs are used with trees.

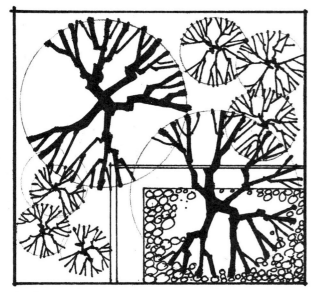

bad

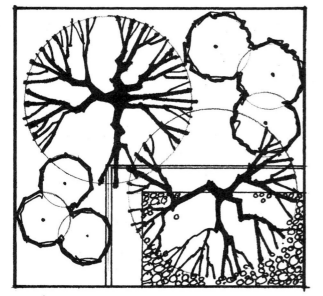

good

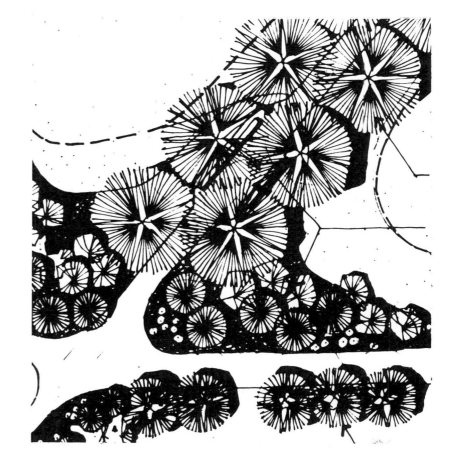

6 Ground Covers

Ground covers include low, creeping plant materials and unmaintained and maintained grassy surfaces. They form a continuous background in plan drawing.

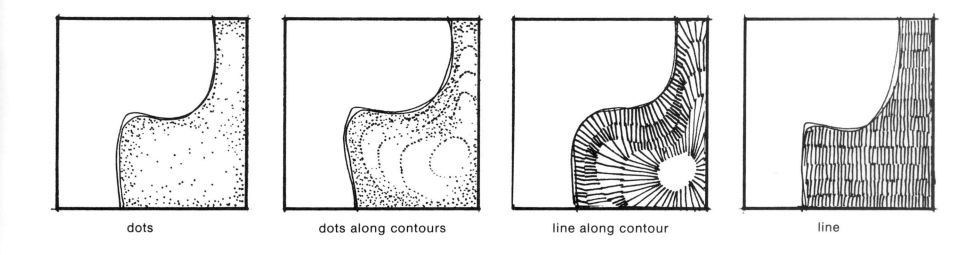

| dots | dots along contours | line along contour | line |

Texture is the combination of lines.

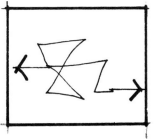

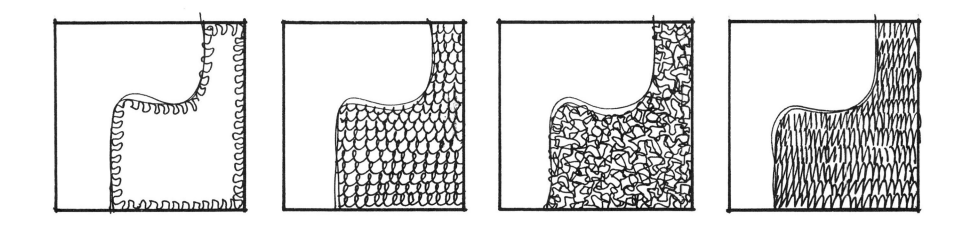

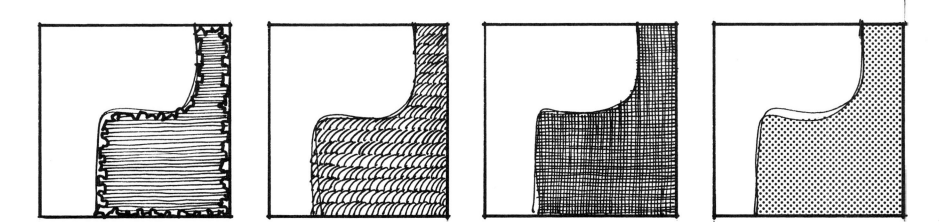

Textures of ground covers should be carefully selected to blend with other symbols. Their intensity should be even, and their line width should be consistent. Avoid varying textures in the same drawing. Excessive differentiation tends to increase the complexity of the plan image and to confuse the viewers.

Ground covers and grass are background materials. A plan drawing without background materials tends to overemphasize the elements (trees or buildings, for example), resulting in a spotty drawing. Background material deemphasizes the individuality of these parts and brings them together harmoniously.

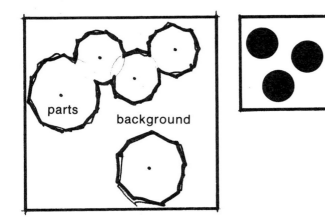

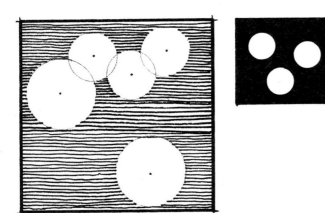

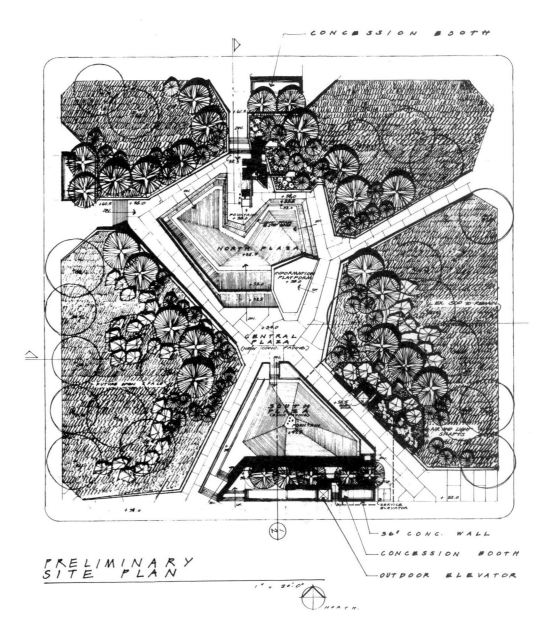

PRELIMINARY
SITE PLAN

1" = 20'0"

46

plan view

dense
branches
to define
edge

elevation

level 1

level 2

level 3

level 4

avoid

Overlapping branch symbols should be carefully spaced so that they do not interfere or block the other symbols underneath them. It is very important for the viewers to complete the edges of these symbols visually. Overlapped edges should be drawn with a thinner line to minimize their complexity.

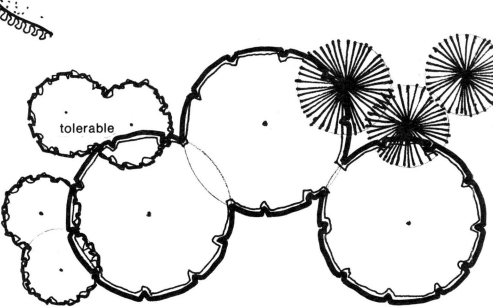

tolerable

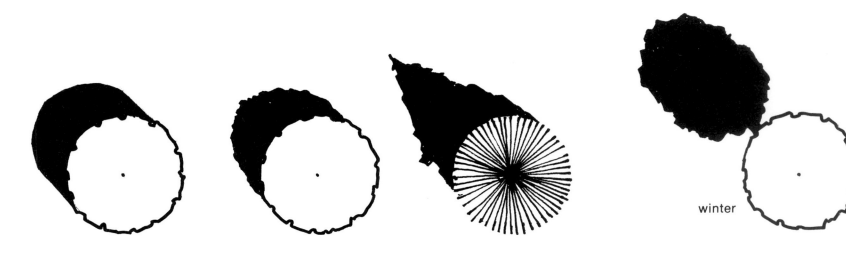

winter

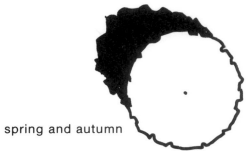

spring and autumn

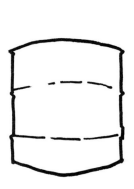

summer

Avoid shadows shaped like an oil drum. The top of a tree is not flat.

The canopy of a tree is usually rounded, with the center as its high point. The shadow of the tree should be longer in the center and gradually slope toward the edges.

Evergreens have a conical profile. The shadow of an evergreen is long and pointed. It has a triangular shape.

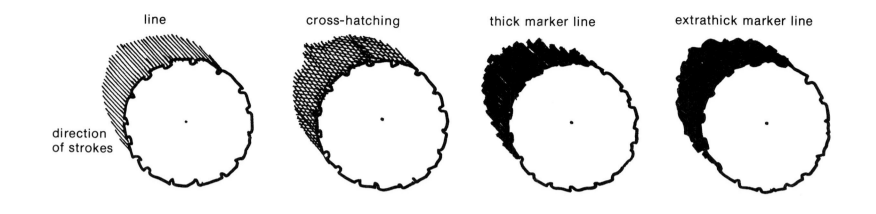

line   cross-hatching   thick marker line   extrathick marker line

direction
of strokes

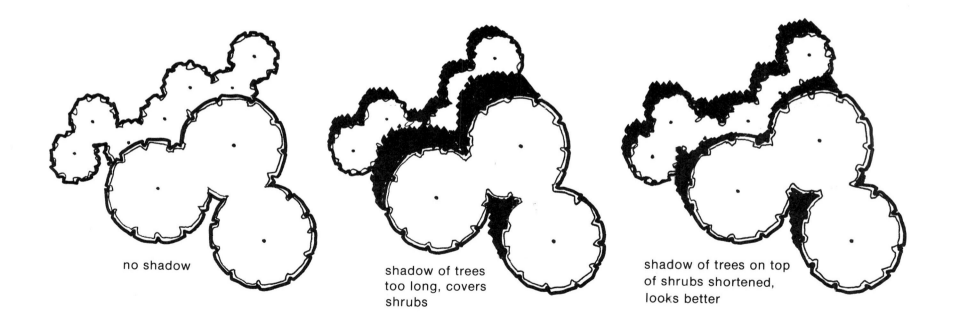

no shadow

shadow of trees
too long, covers
shrubs

shadow of trees on top
of shrubs shortened,
looks better

8 Pavements

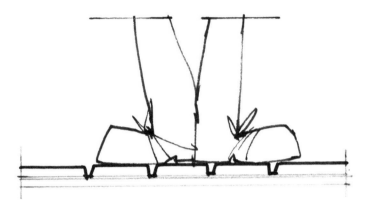

outline

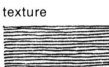

dots

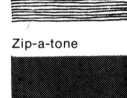

texture

Zip-a-tone

Pavement, like ground cover, can bring parts together. It is also a kind of background material in plan drawing. Pavement symbols vary from project to project. Most of these symbols are simplified expressions of the real thing. They indicate the surface condition as well as the pattern. The amount of detail and texture depends on the size and scale of the drawing. For example, showing individual brick paving on a 200:1-scale plan is not only inappropriate but a waste of time. Use your common sense and creativity in selecting these symbols.

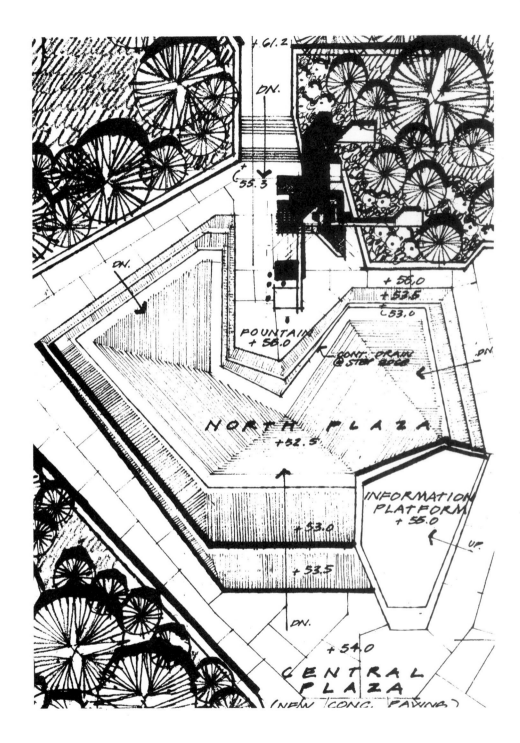

typical pavement symbols

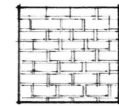
tile

brick

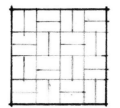
brick/tile

brick

concrete

concrete

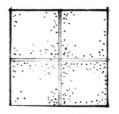
stone

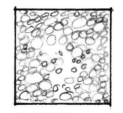
aggregate

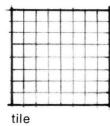
rock

stone

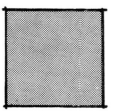
concrete with joints

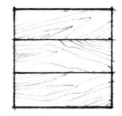
wood

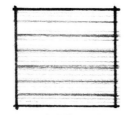
wood (Zip-a-tone)

concrete (Zip-a-tone)

stone (Zip-a-tone)

9 Water

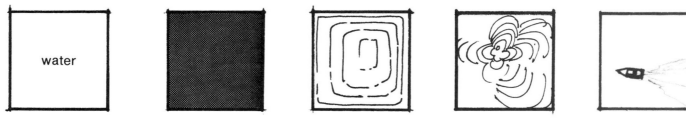

| label | Zip-a-tone | show fathom line | show ripple | show waves |

coastline

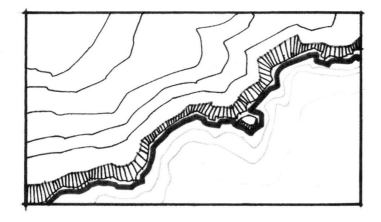

swimming pool

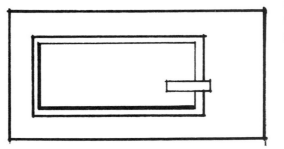

Water is usually identified by its edge. The edge defines the limit of the water body and also gives a hint to the viewer of its function and characteristics. There is no need to reinforce this nonverbal communication by introducing redundant graphic symbols—a well-defined edge and possibly color are all that are needed.

The water in this example is rendered dark to bring out the contrast between it and the land.

The water in this example is rendered by a few lines drawn parallel to the shoreline. These lines indicate the gradual change in water depth.

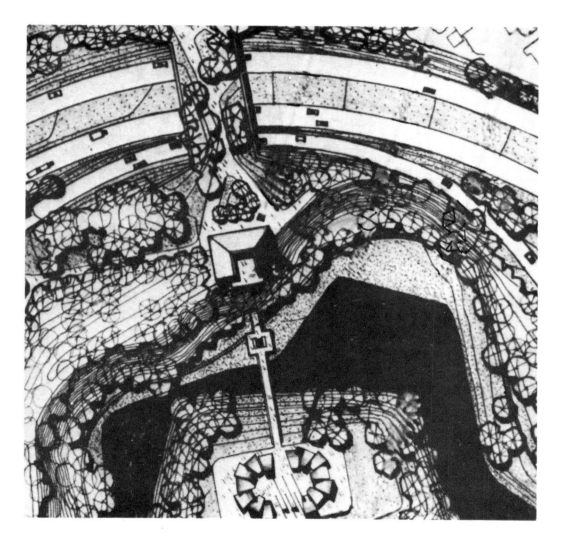

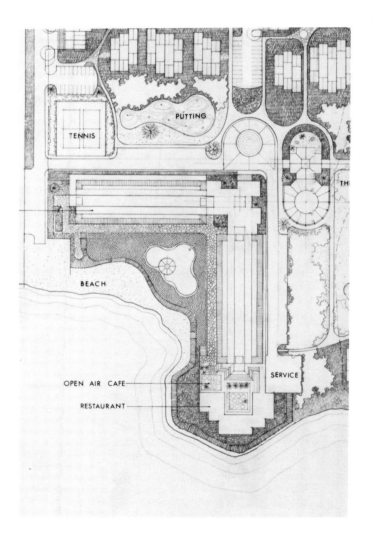

10 Cars

Cars, like boats and people, are decorative elements in plan drawing. They play supporting roles and enhance the quality of plan drawing. They are scale indicators as well as cues to the function of the design.

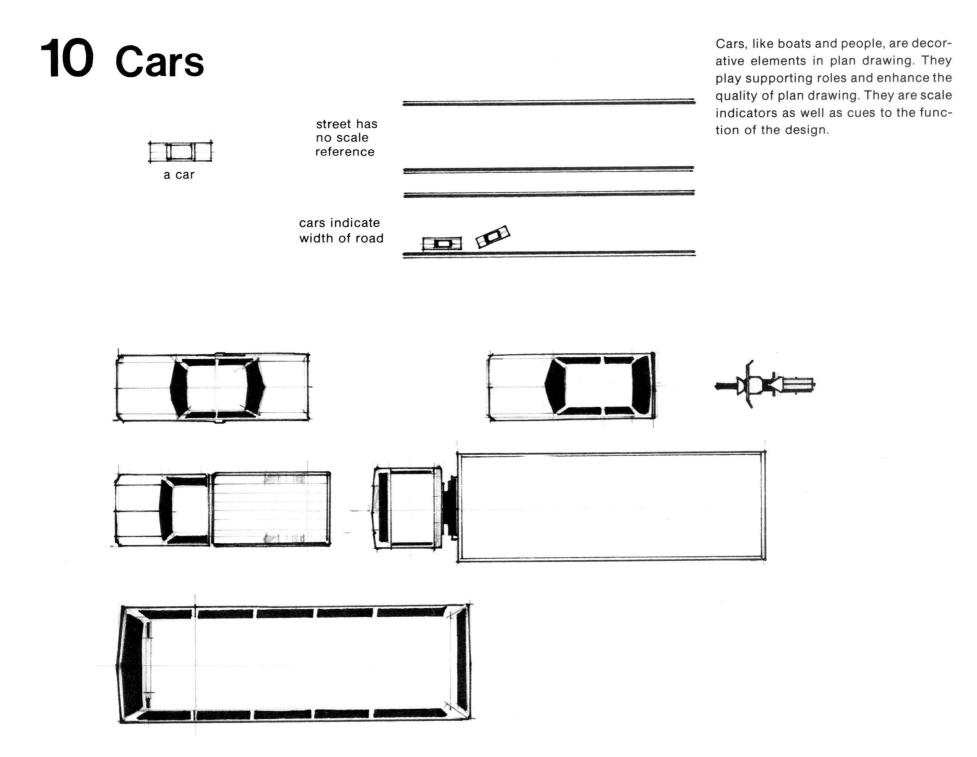

a car

street has
no scale
reference

cars indicate
width of road

simple, symbolic

amount of detail

complex, real

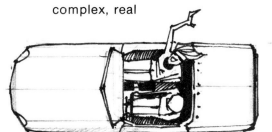

Cars are not part of the design. They should not be over-done, because excessive details will draw attention away from the design. They should be drawn to scale, however, and placed in accordance with traffic regulations.

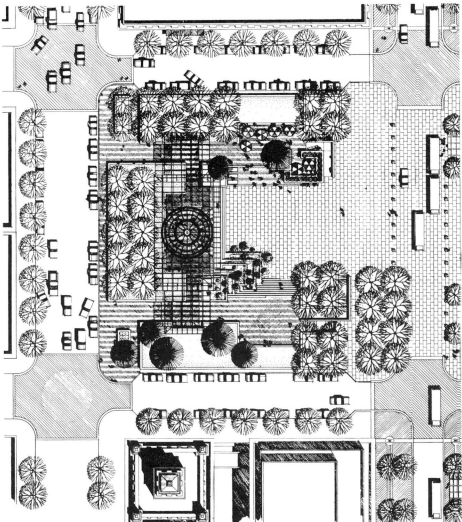

11 Roads

width of road

A single line does not have a strong spatial edge. Double lines are more defined and are often used to indicate curb cuts.

curb

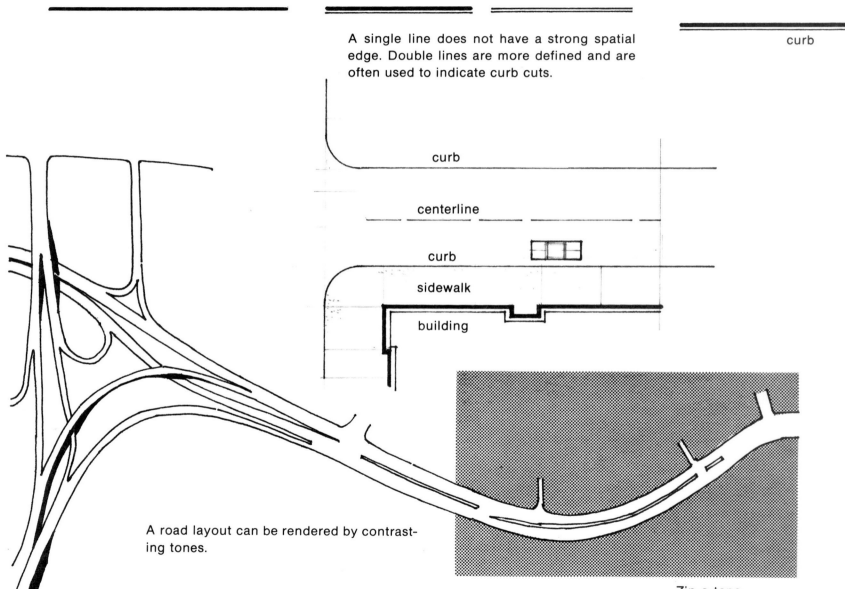

curb

centerline

curb

sidewalk

building

A road layout can be rendered by contrasting tones.

Zip-a-tone

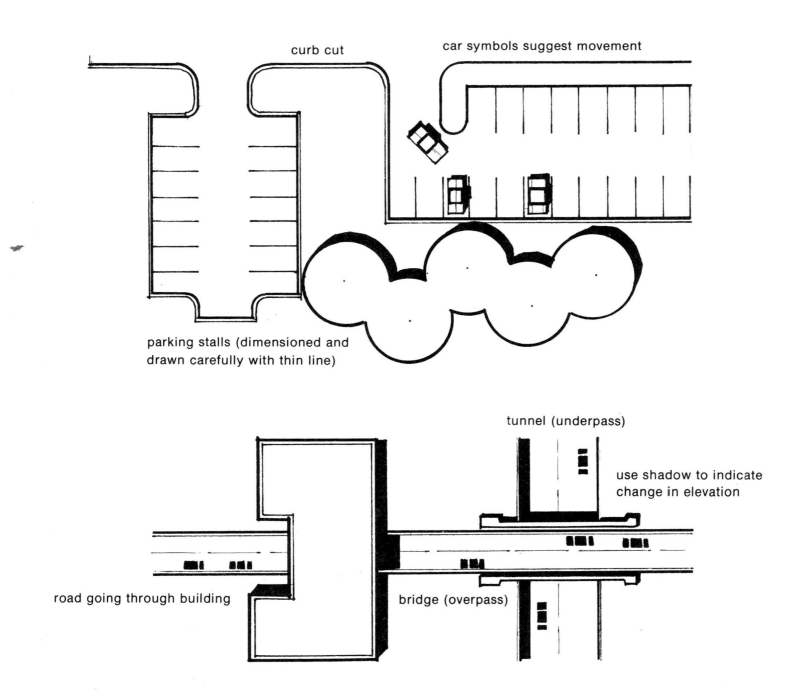

curb cut

car symbols suggest movement

parking stalls (dimensioned and
drawn carefully with thin line)

tunnel (underpass)

use shadow to indicate
change in elevation

road going through building

bridge (overpass)

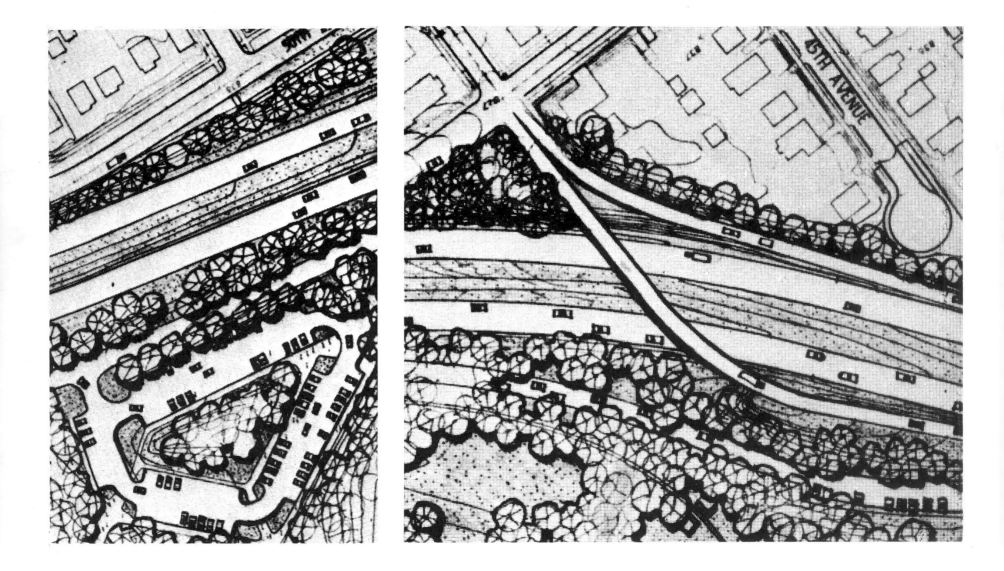

Section and elevation drawings are more realistic and easier to understand than plan drawings. They not only show the horizontal dimension but also the vertical dimension. With the cue of height the viewer can relate to the design more easily than with the two-dimensional plan.

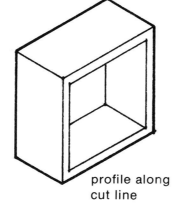

object

cut line

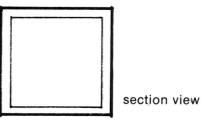

profile along
cut line

section view

Construction detail shows the construction materials, the methods of construction, and the dimensioning.

Landscape shows the change in topography.

Landscape and building show the location of the house and the indoor/outdoor relationship.

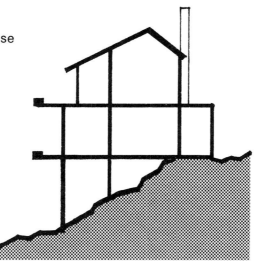

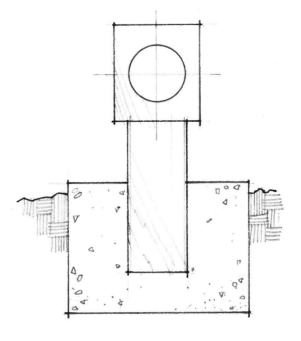

Elevation is a kind of orthographic projection (side view). The viewer is usually perpendicular to the frontal plane of the object. There are some exceptions. The picture plane and the frontal plane are parallel. The elevation is taken from a horizontal point of view, assuming that the viewer is at normal eye level (5 to 6 feet above ground). A section elevation shows not only the profile of the cut line but also the image behind this line (plane).

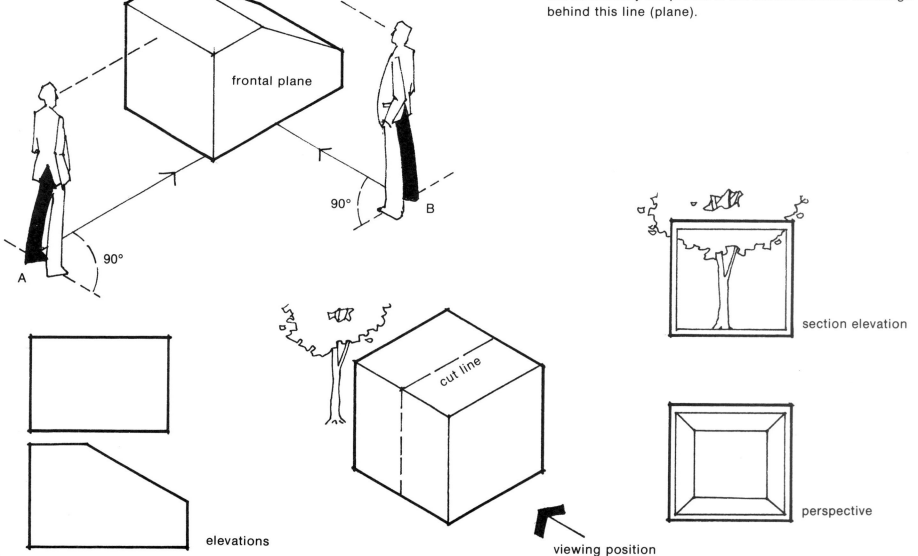

frontal plane

90°

90°

A

B

elevations

cut line

viewing position

section elevation

perspective

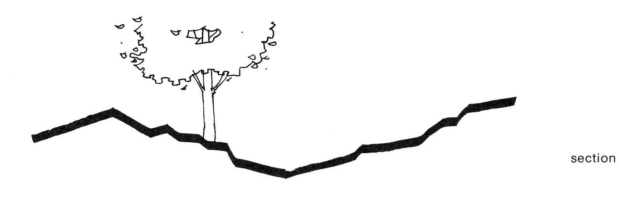

section

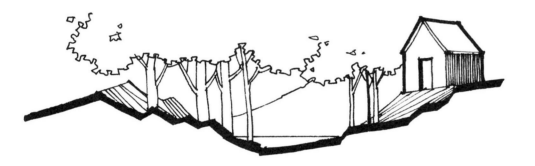

section elevation

section perspective

61

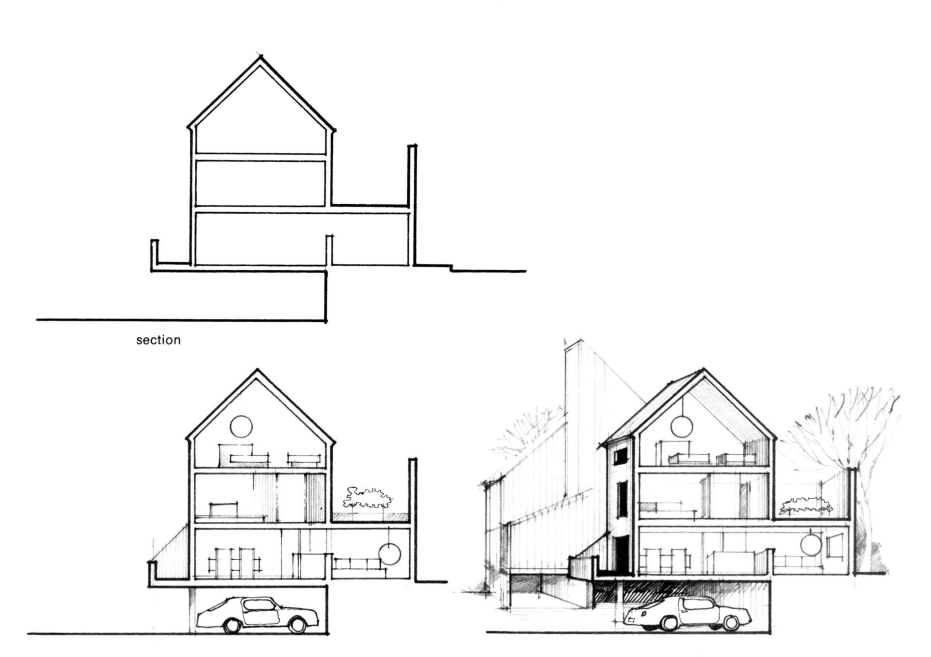

section

section elevation

section perspective

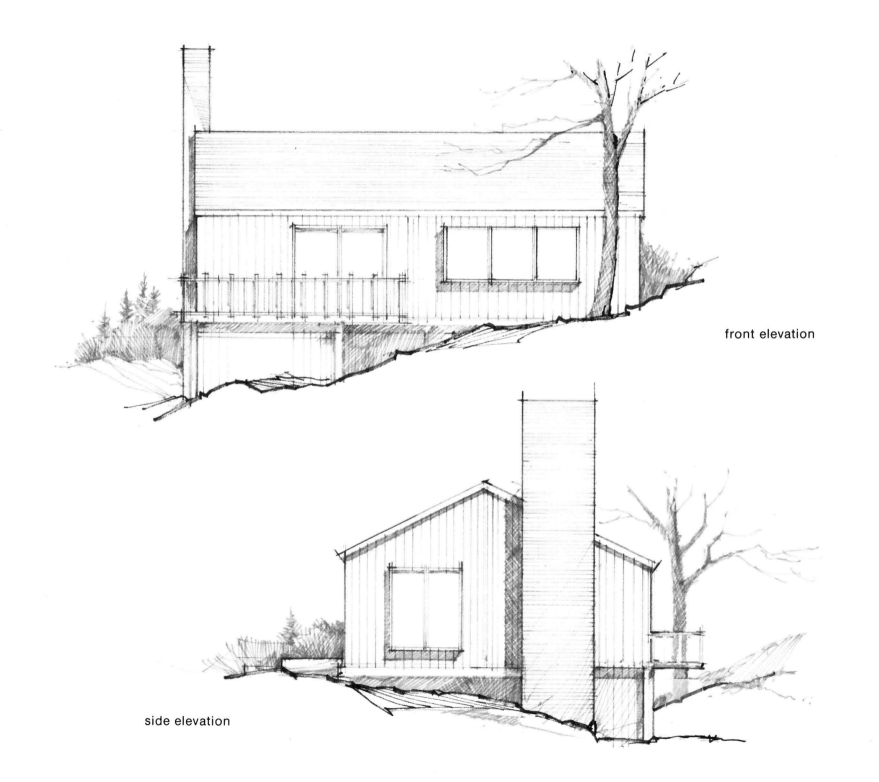

front elevation

side elevation

13 Line Weight and Vertical Exaggeration

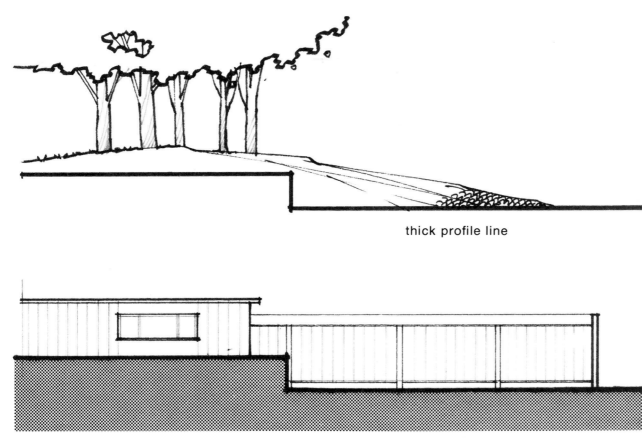

thick profile line

Zip-a-tone

Section and elevation are two-dimensional drawings. They do not show perspective and therefore do not give the viewer the illusion of depth. Varying line widths are the key depth reference in section and elevation drawing. The cut line is usually the thickest line because it is closest to the viewer. Heavy lines give the drawing a steady foundation. Objects in the distance should be drawn with thinner lines, but the profile of these objects should be outlined with a medium line for better definition. Zip-a-tone is often used to mask the foundation in order to maintain a consistent base for all section and elevation drawing despite the variation on the surface.

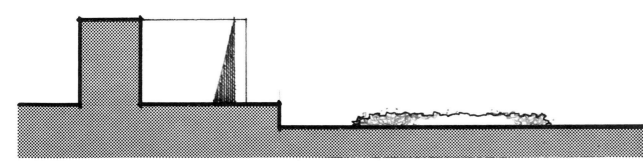

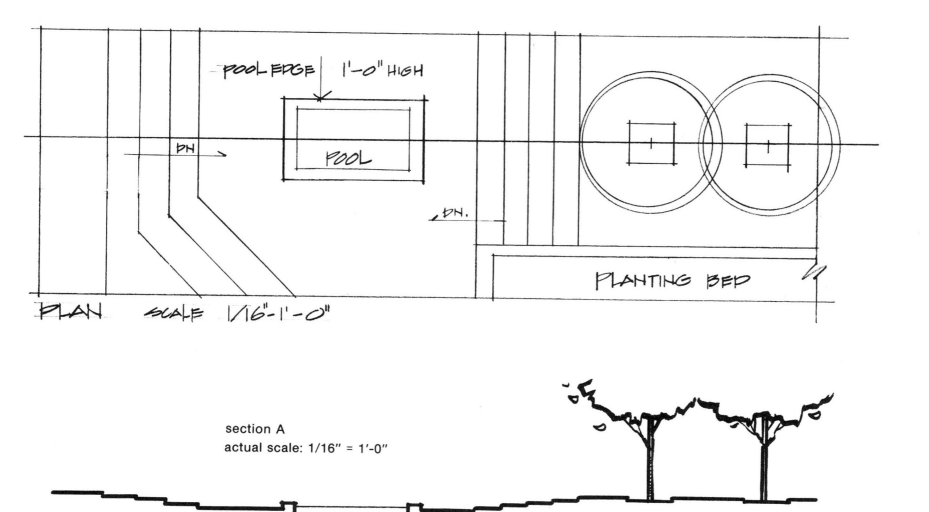

POOL EDGE | 1'-0" HIGH

POOL

PLANTING BED

DN

DN.

PLAN   SCALE 1/16"-1'-0"

section A
actual scale: 1/16" = 1'-0"

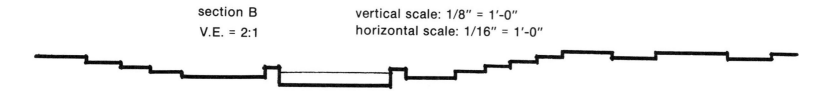

section B
V.E. = 2:1

vertical scale: 1/8" = 1'-0"
horizontal scale: 1/16" = 1'-0"

The intent of section and elevation drawings is to show the change in the vertical dimension. The span of the horizontal distance is often so great that it makes the change seem insignificant. Vertical exaggeration is used to enlarge the height in order to amplify its effect. It is a distorted image. Vertical exaggeration is frequently used in regional sections to show the relationship between subregions. It is not appropriate in man-made environments to exaggerate the vertical dimension.

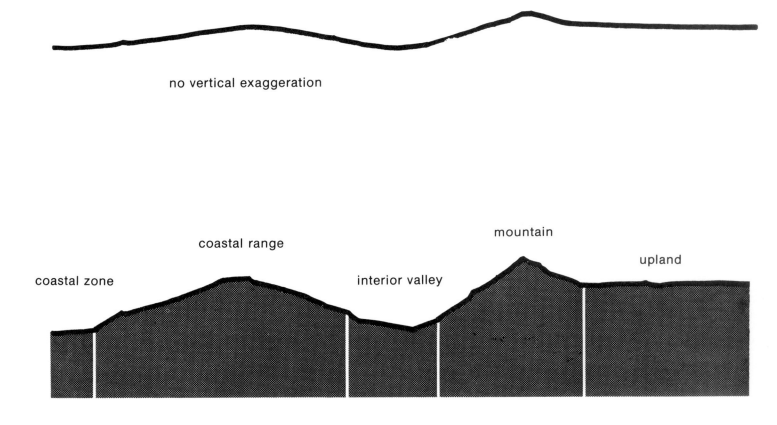

no vertical exaggeration

coastal zone coastal range mountain upland interior valley

vertical exaggeration

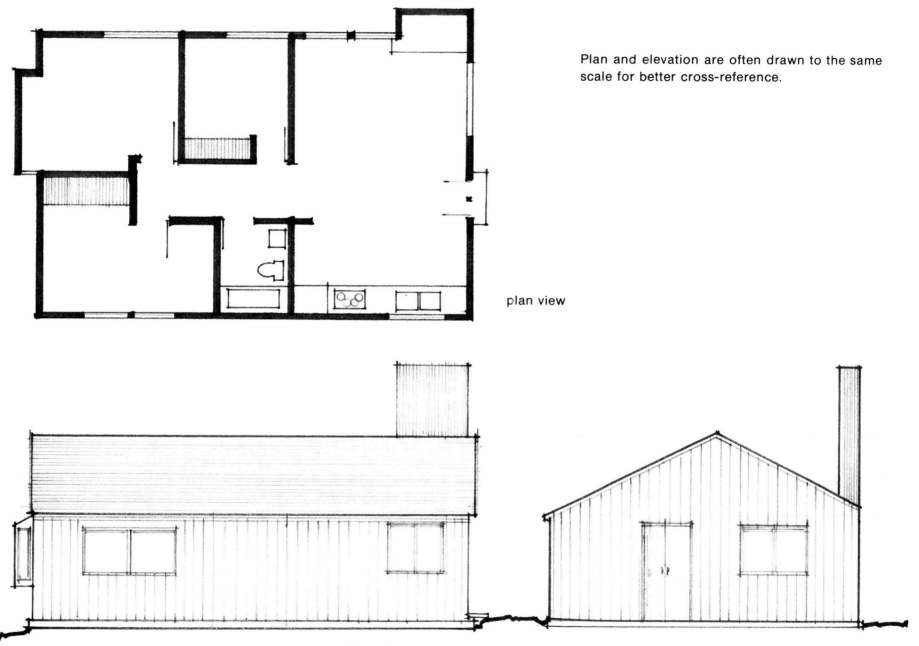

Plan and elevation are often drawn to the same scale for better cross-reference.

plan view

front view

side view

14 Plant Materials

Symbols in section and elevation drawings can be classified into four major groups: buildings, plants, design elements, and supporting elements.

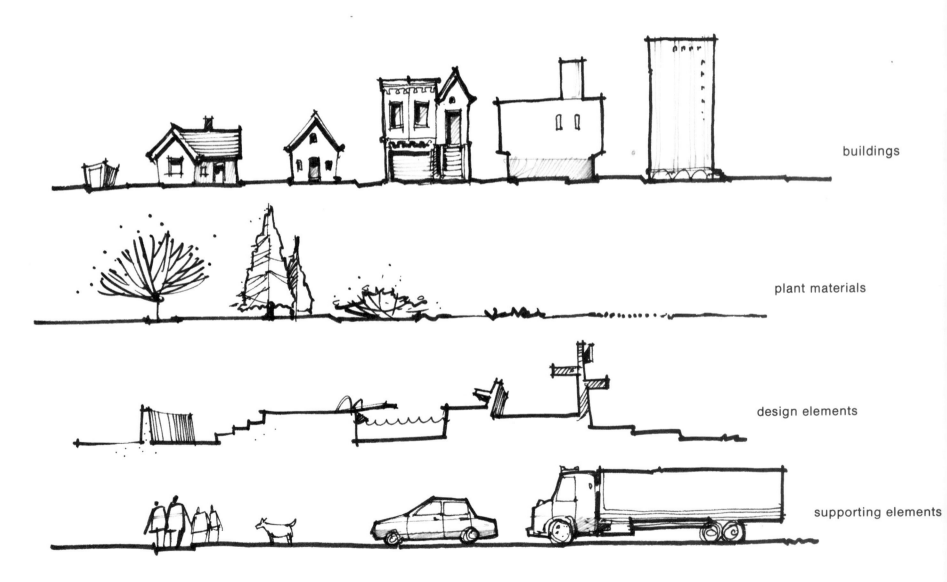

buildings

plant materials

design elements

supporting elements

basic tree forms

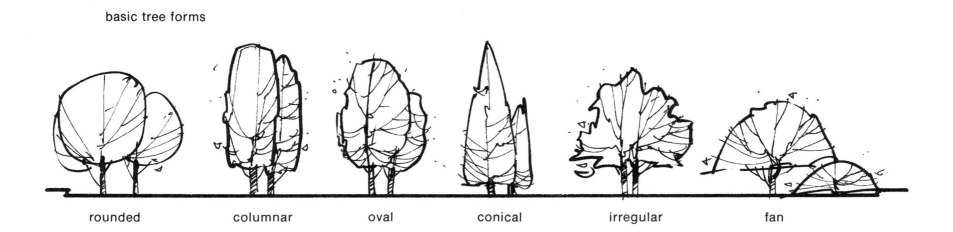

rounded   columnar   oval   conical   irregular   fan

ways to draw trees

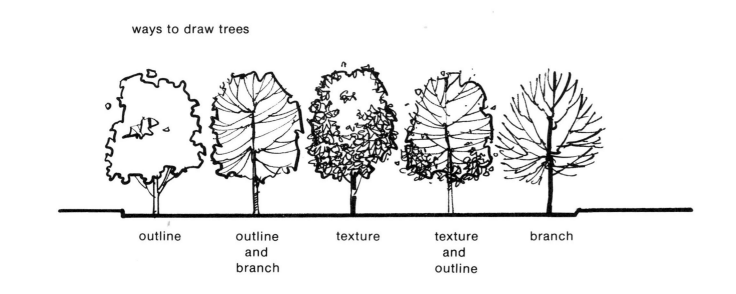

outline   outline
and
branch   texture   texture
and
outline   branch

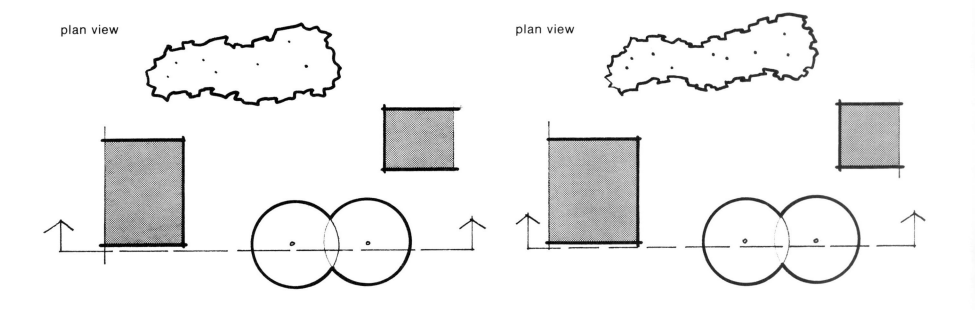

elevation

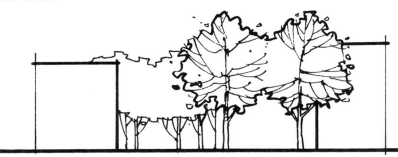

Trees in the background are drawn with a thin line. They are on the same scale as the rest of the frontal plane, because it is an orthographic projection.

perspective

Background trees are smaller because of the perspective image.

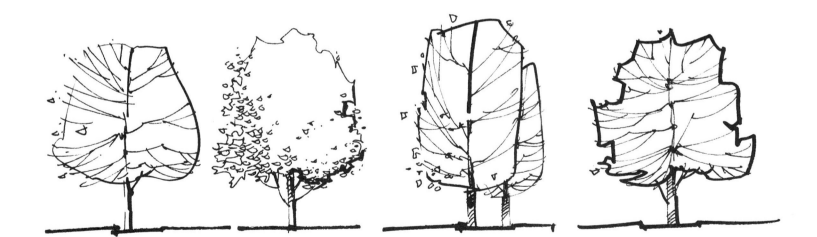

examples of evergreen trees

foreground trees

These symbols are for framing. The trees in the foreground should have more detail. The outline of closeup materials should be drawn with a thick line.

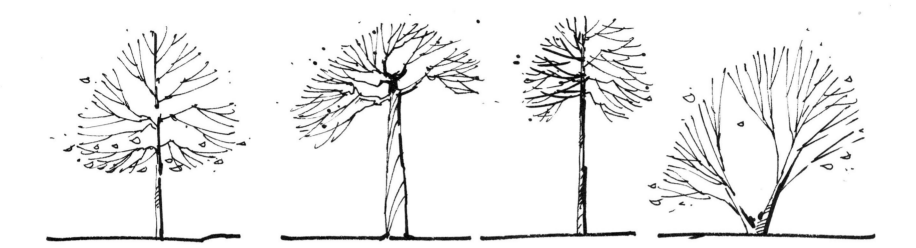

typical branch-type tree symbols

Outline the tree with a thin pencil line.

Sketch the major branches and reinforce the trunk.

Fill in the rest of the branches. Add a few stipples as an indication of motion.

The technique of drawing shrubs is similar to that of trees. A combination of outline and branch is the most popular shrub symbol. Textures should represent leaves as well as ground cover.

basic shrub forms

oval, rounded   fan   low, creeping   lawn

outline and branch

texture

74

texture

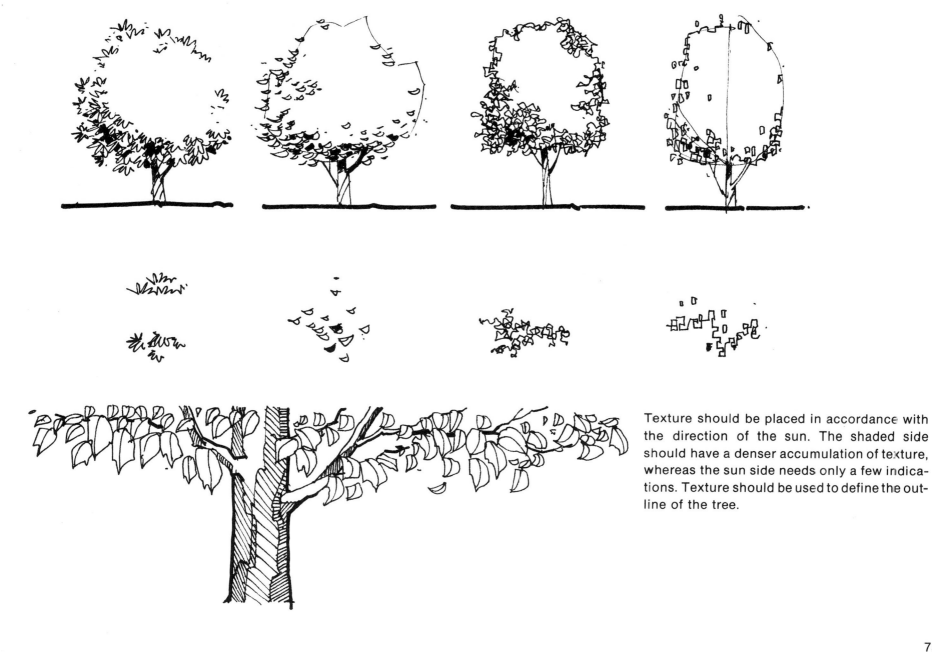

Texture should be placed in accordance with the direction of the sun. The shaded side should have a denser accumulation of texture, whereas the sun side needs only a few indications. Texture should be used to define the outline of the tree.

15 Shadows

Shadow in section and elevation drawings emphasizes the illusion of depth. It should be used along with different line widths to maximize the three-dimensional effect. The angle and intensity of the shadows should be consistent throughout the entire drawing. Shadow is usually darker than shade.

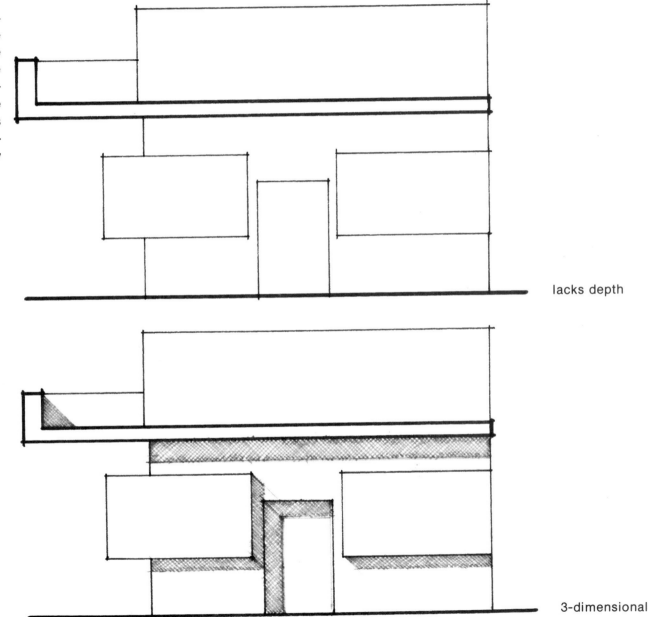

lacks depth

3-dimensional

section elevation
before construction

after construction

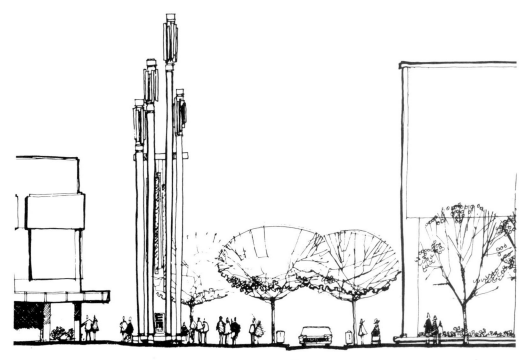

OAK ENTRY AT BROADWAY

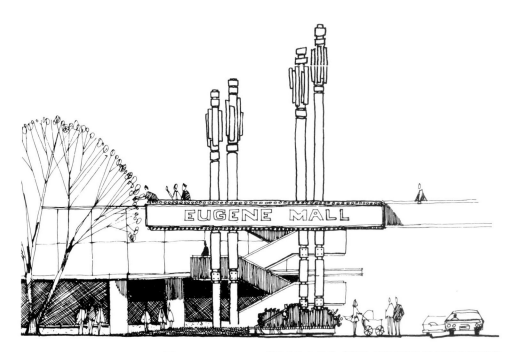

CHARNELTON OVER-WALK AT BROADWAY

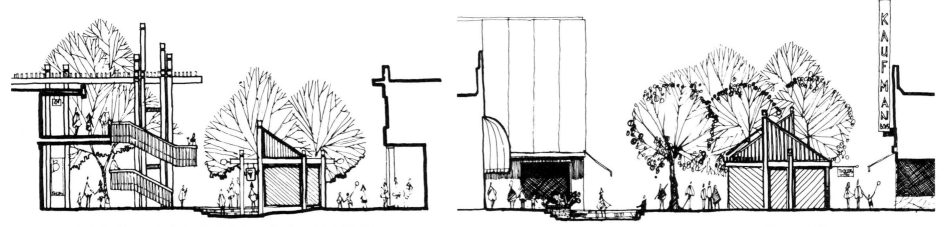

STAIRS TO 2ND LEVEL SHOPS

MALL SHOPS

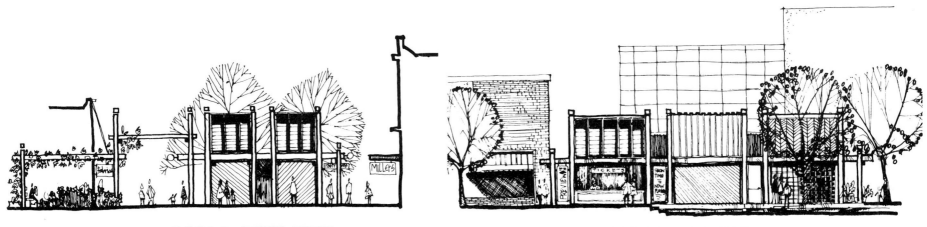

MALL TOILETS

MALL SHOPS

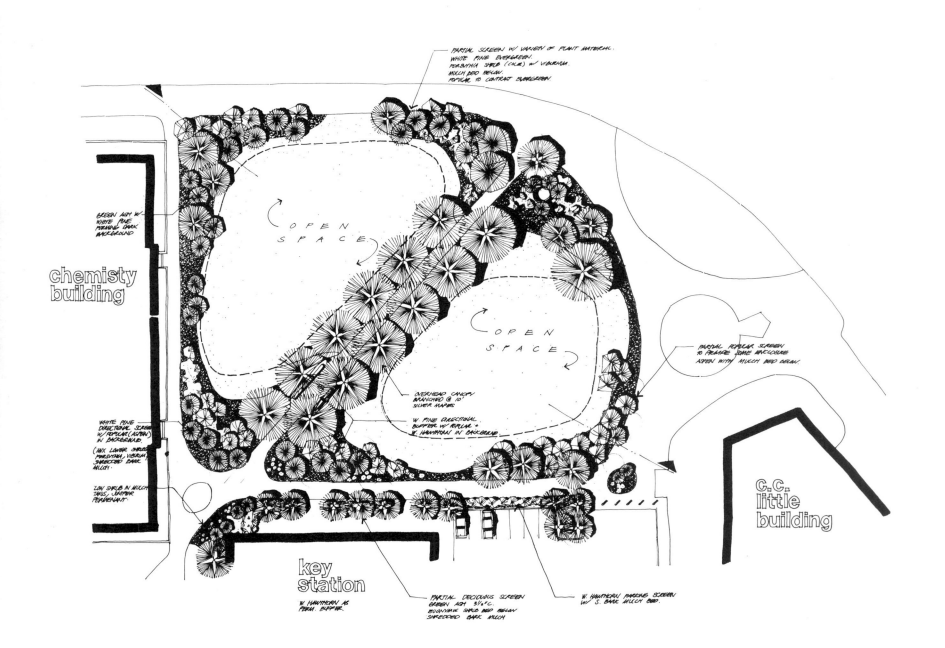

PARTIAL SCREEN W/ VARIETY OF PLANT MATERIAL.
WHITE PINE EVERGREEN.
FORSYTHIA SHRUB (COLOR) W/ VIBURNUM.
MULCH BED BEGIN.
POPULAR TO CONTRAST EVERGREEN.

GREEN ASH W/
WHITE PINE
FORMING DARK
BACKGROUND

chemisty
building

OPEN
SPACE

OPEN
SPACE

PARTIAL POPULAR SCREEN
TO PROVIDE SOME ENCLOSURE
ASPEN WITH MULCH BED BEGIN.

OVERHEAD CANOPY
BRANCHED @ 10'
SILVER MAPLES

WHITE PINE
DIRECTIONAL SCREEN
W/ POPULAR (ASPEN)
IN BACKGROUND.

(MIX LOWER SHRUB
FORSYTHIA, VIBURNUM,
SHREDDED BARK
MULCH.

LOW SHRUB IN MULCH
TAXUS, JUNIPER
PERMANENT.

W. PINE DIRECTIONAL
BUFFER W/ POPULAR +
W. HAWTHORN IN BACKGROUND.

C.C.
little
building

key
station

W. HAWTHORN AS
PERM. BUFFER.

PARTIAL DECIDUOUS SCREEN
GREEN ASH 3¼"C.
EUONYMUS SHRUB BED BEGIN
SHREDDED BARK MULCH.

W. HAWTHORN PARKING SCREEN
W/ S. BARK MULCH BED.

80

9

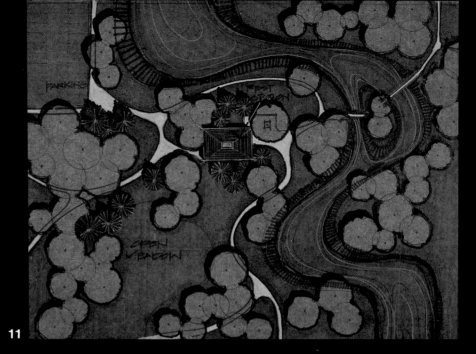

11

10

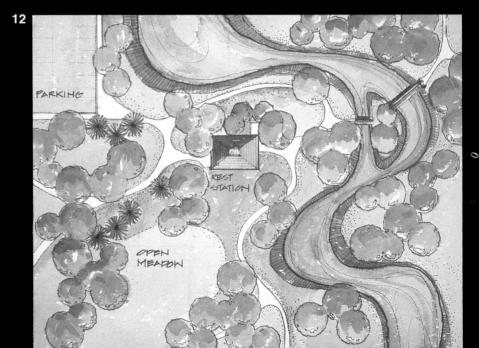

12

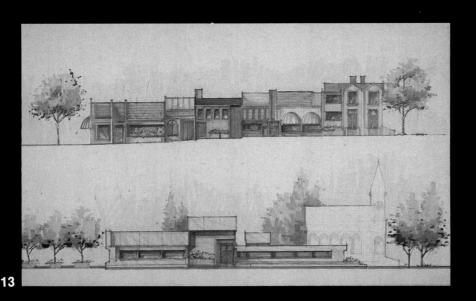

13

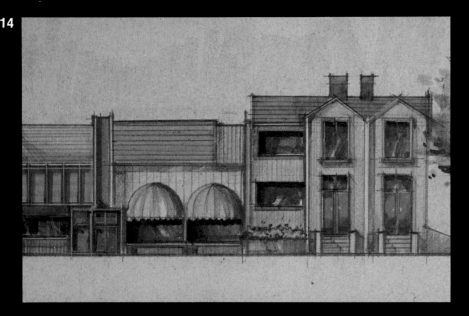

14

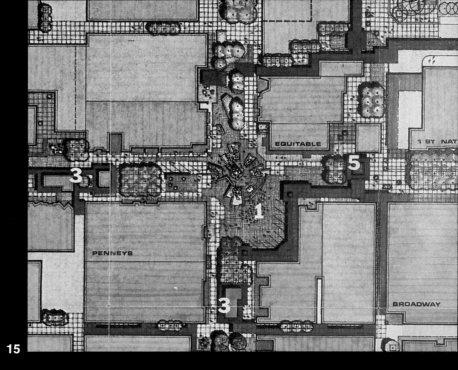

15

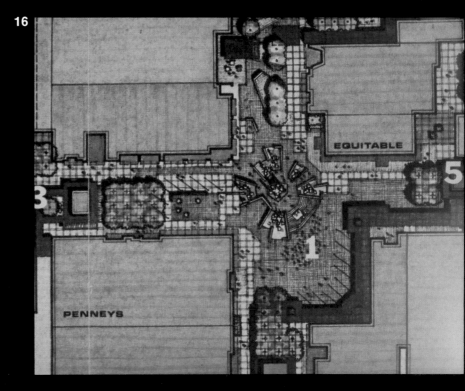

16

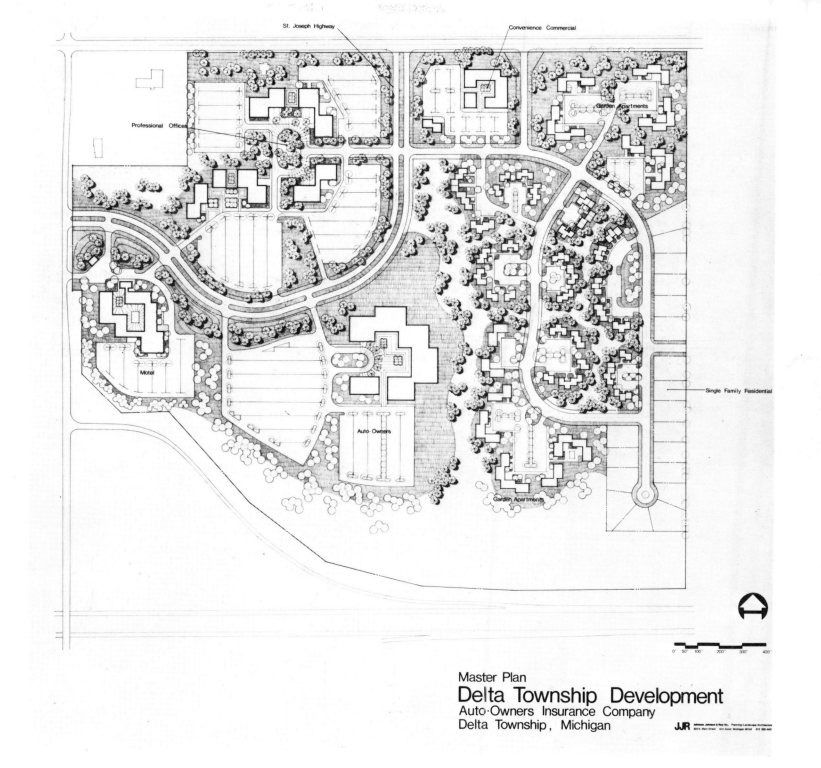

St. Joseph Highway

Convenience Commercial

Professional Offices

Garden Apartments

Single Family Residential

Motel

Auto-Owners

Garden Apartments

Master Plan
Delta Township Development
Auto-Owners Insurance Company
Delta Township, Michigan

JJR Johnson, Johnson & Roy/Inc. Planning/Landscape Architecture

0' 50' 100'   200'   300'   400'

FIRE STATION

RESTAURANT

THEATER

MERCY ST.

BUS STOP

CITY HALL ADDITION

CITY HALL

SUNKEN PLAZA

BELL TOWER

POLICE STATION

LIBRARY

PIONEER PARK

LIBRARY ADDITION

PARKING STRUCTURE

BAILEY AVE.

CASTRO STREET

CHURCH STREET

MOUNTAIN VIEW CIVIC CENTER
MOUNTAIN VIEW, CALIFORNIA

NORTH
SCALE: 1' = 40'-0'

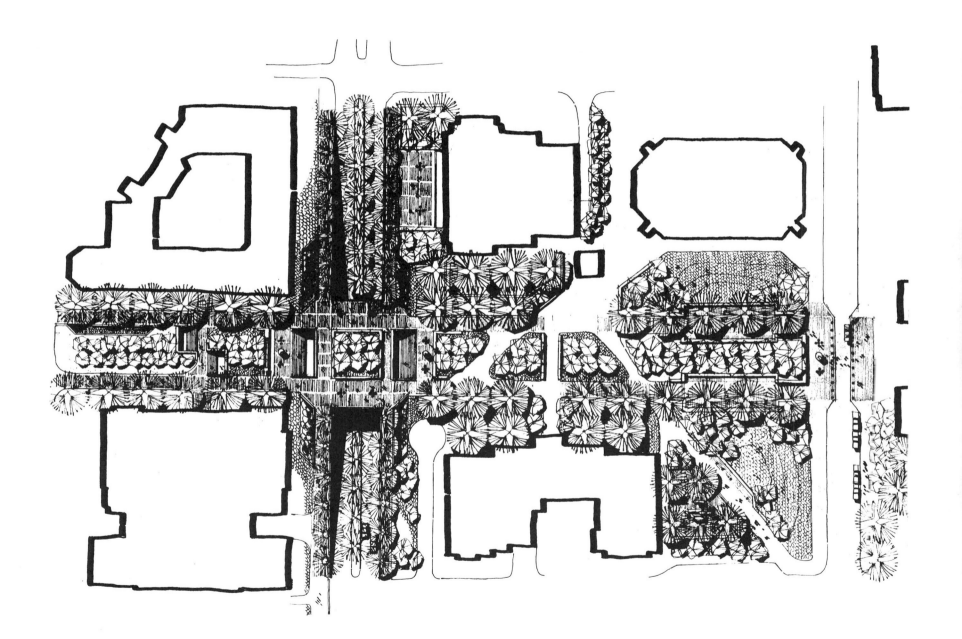

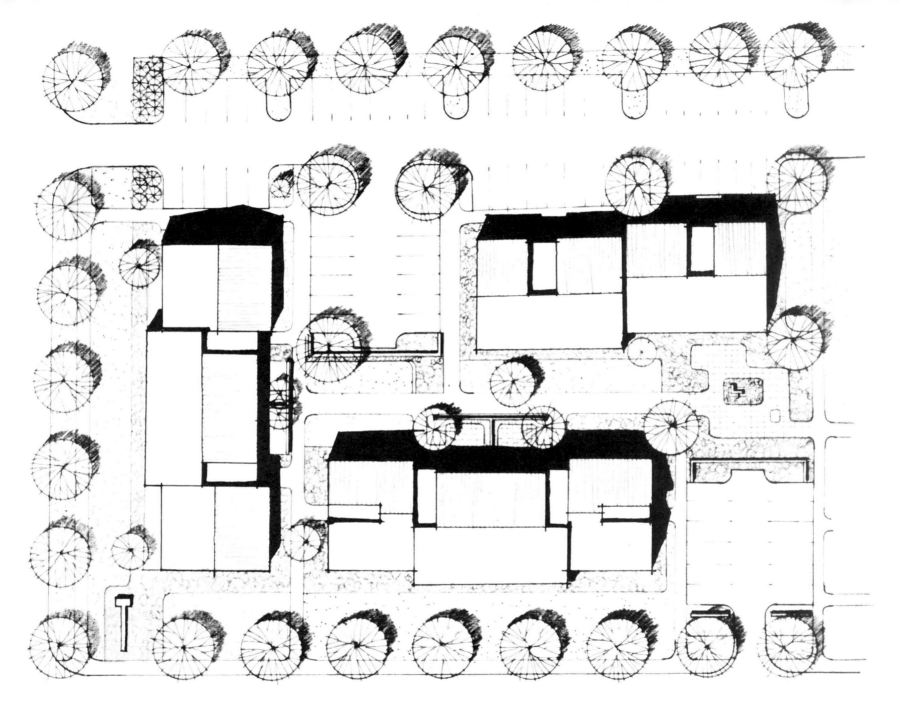

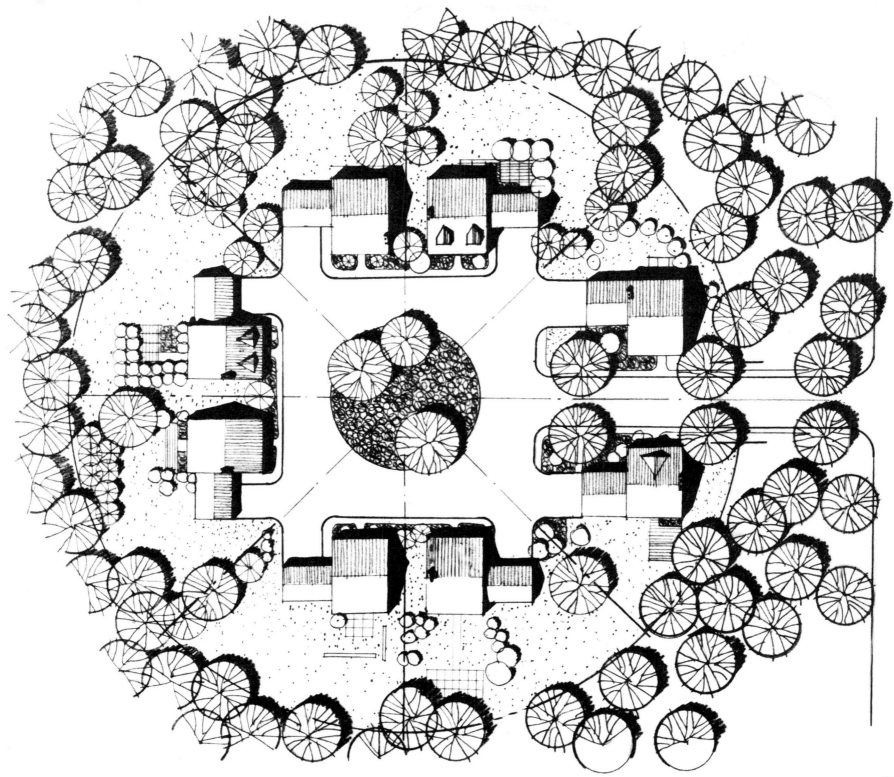

85

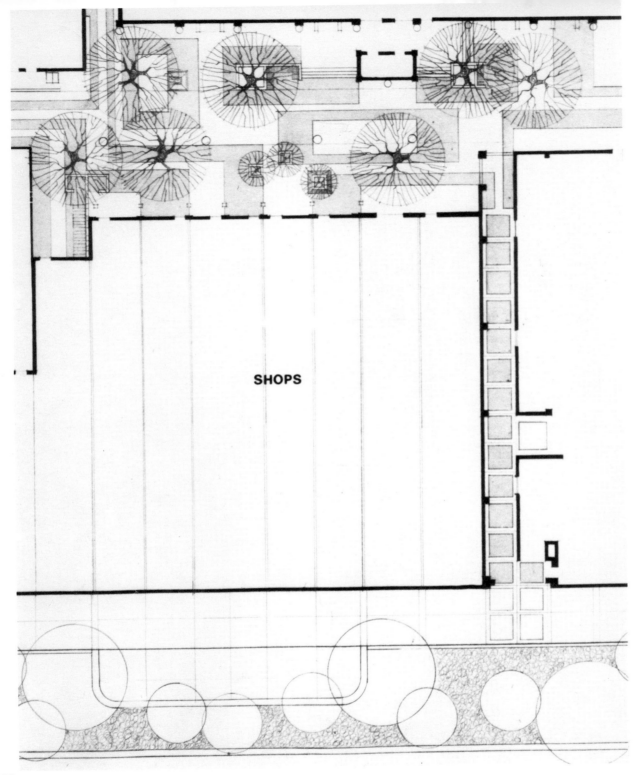

SHOPS

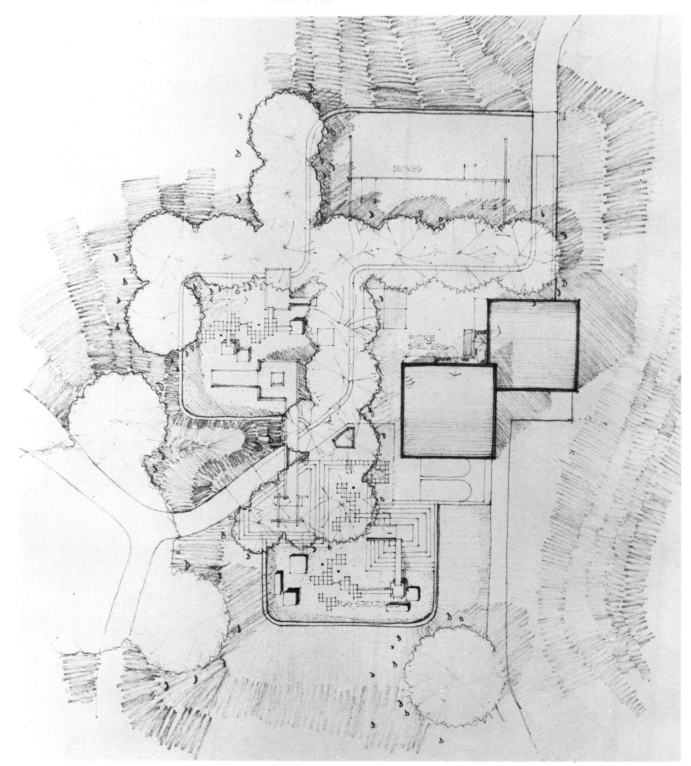

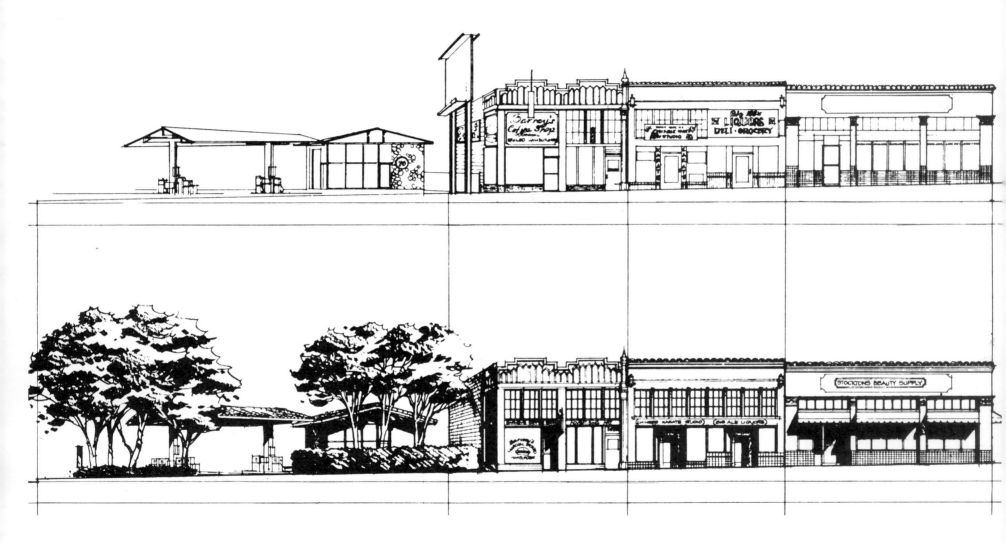

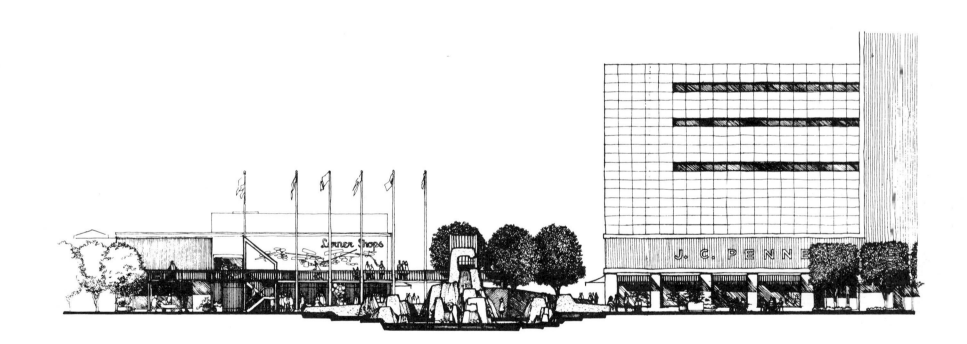

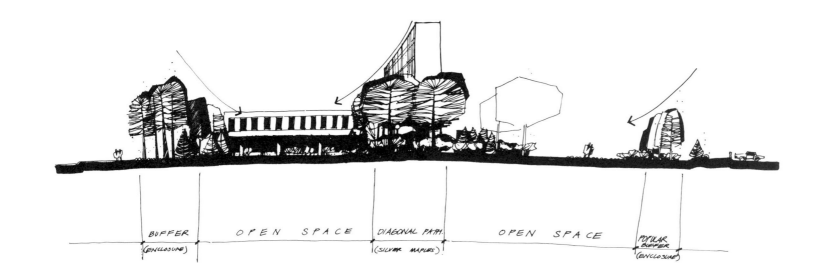

BUFFER   O P E N   S P A C E   DIAGONAL PATH   O P E N   S P A C E   POPLAR BUFFER

(ENCLOSURE)   (SILVER MAPLES)   (ENCLOSURE)

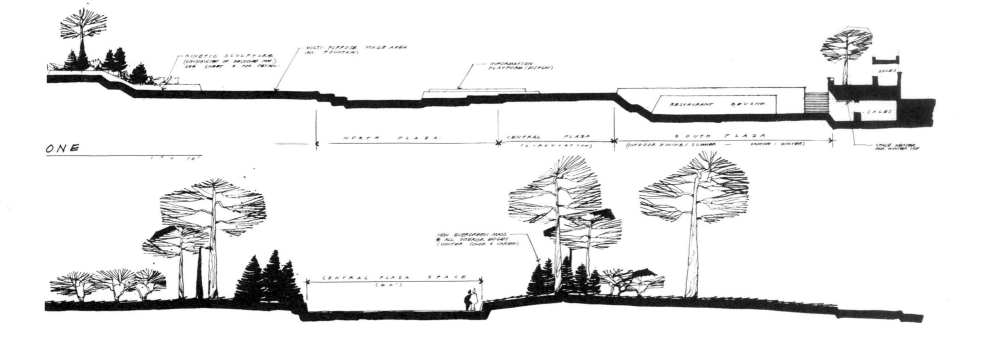

KINETIC SCULPTURE
(CONSTRUCTED OF RECYCLED MAT.)
SEE SHEET 6 FOR DETAIL.

MULTI-PURPOSE STAGE AREA
(INC. FOUNTAIN)

INFORMATION
PLATFORM (DISPLAY)

SALES

RESTAURANT   BEYOND.

SALES

ONE

1" = 10'

NORTH PLAZA   CENTRAL PLAZA   SOUTH PLAZA

(CIRCULATION)   (OUTDOOR DINING / SUMMER — SKATING · WINTER)

SPACE HEATER
FOR WINTER USE

NEW EVERGREEN MASS
@ ALL INTERIOR EDGES
(WINTER COLOR & VARIETY)

CENTRAL PLAZA   SPACE
(90')

TWO

1" = 10'

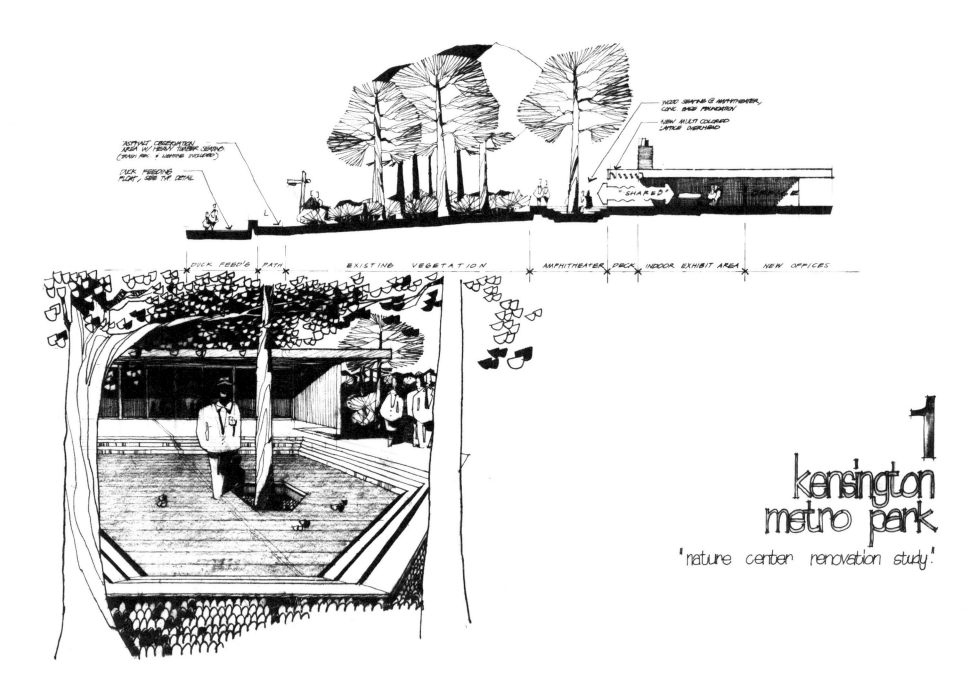

ASPHALT OBSERVATION
AREA W/ HEAVY TIMBER SEATING.
(TRASH REC. & LIGHTING INCLUDED)

DUCK FEEDING
FLOAT, SEE TYP. DETAIL

WOOD SEATING @ AMPHITHEATER,
CONC. BASE FOUNDATION

NEW MULTI COLORED
LATTICE OVERHEAD

"SHARED"

DUCK FEED'G PATH   EXISTING VEGETATION   AMPHITHEATER DECK   INDOOR EXHIBIT AREA   NEW OFFICES

1
kensington
metro park

'nature center renovation study'

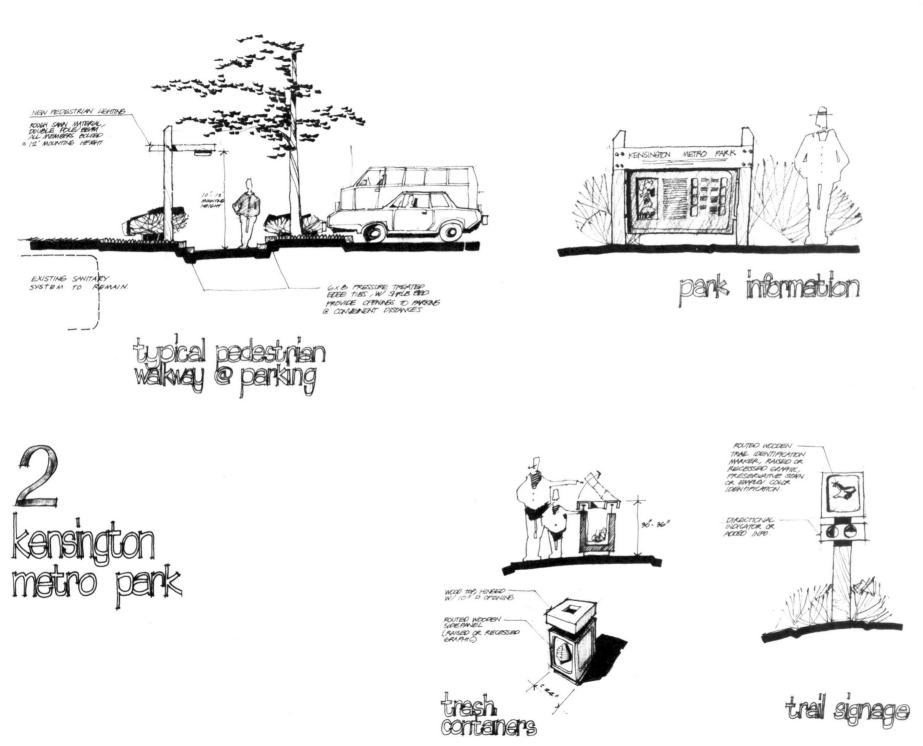

NEW PEDESTRIAN LIGHTING
ROUGH SAWN MATERIAL,
DOUBLE POLE BEAM
ALL MEMBERS BOLTED
≈ 12' MOUNTING HEIGHT

10'-12'
MOUNTING
HEIGHT

EXISTING SANITARY
SYSTEM TO REMAIN.

6 X 8 PRESSURE TREATED
EDGE TIES / W SHRUB BED
PROVIDE OPENINGS TO PARKING
@ CONVENIENT DISTANCES

typical pedestrian
walkway @ parking

KENSINGTON METRO PARK

park information

2
kensington
metro park

30"-36"

WOOD TOP, HINGED
W/ 10" Ø OPENING

ROUTED WOODEN
SIDE PANEL
(RAISED OR RECESSED
GRAPHIC)

24"

trash
containers

ROUTED WOODEN
TRAIL IDENTIFICATION
MARKER, RAISED OR
RECESSED GRAPHIC,
PRESERVATIVE STAIN
OR EMPLOY COLOR
IDENTIFICATION.

DIRECTIONAL
INDICATOR OR
ADDED INFO

trail signage

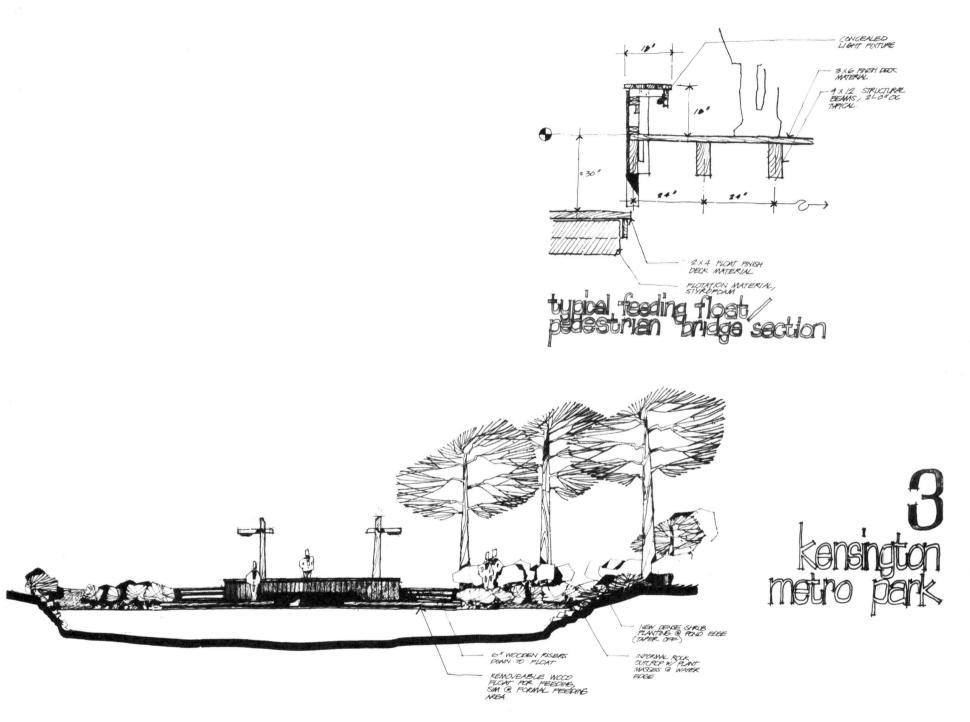

CONCEALED
LIGHT FIXTURE

3 X 6 FINISH DECK
MATERIAL

4 X 12 STRUCTURAL
BEAMS, 2'-0" OC
TYPICAL.

16"

10"

≈ 30"

24"

24"

2 X 4 FLOAT FINISH
DECK MATERIAL

FLOTATION MATERIAL,
STYROFOAM

typical feeding float/
pedestrian bridge section

3

kensington
metro park

NEW DENSE SHRUB
PLANTING @ POND EDGE
(TAPER OFF)

INFORMAL ROCK
OUTCROP W/ PLANT
MASSES @ WATER
EDGE

6" WOODEN RISERS
DOWN TO FLOAT

REMOVEABLE WOOD
FLOAT FOR FEEDING,
SIM. @ FORMAL FEEDING
AREA.

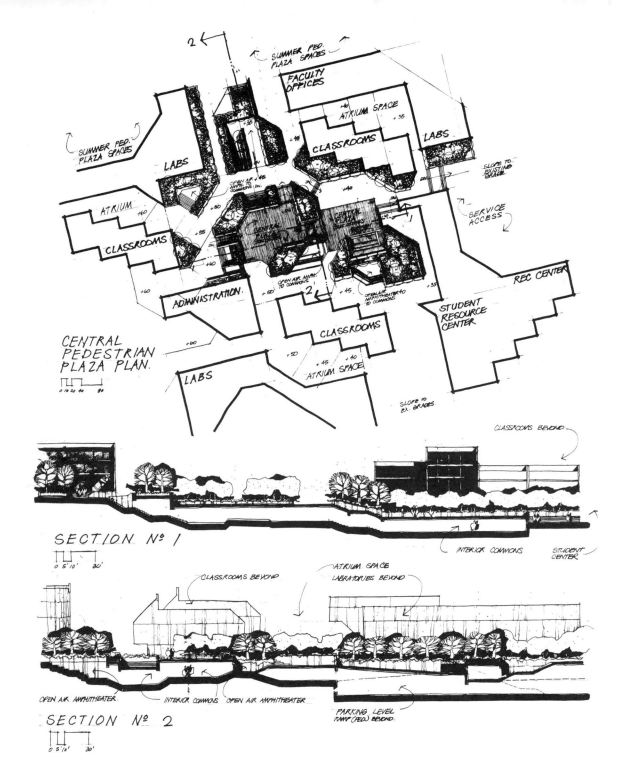

CENTRAL
PEDESTRIAN
PLAZA PLAN.

0 10 20 40   80

FACULTY
OFFICES

SUMMER PED.
PLAZA SPACES

SUMMER PED.
PLAZA SPACES

ATRIUM SPACE

CLASSROOMS

LABS

LABS

SLOPE TO
EXISTING GRADE

SERVICE
ACCESS

ATRIUM

CLASSROOMS

ADMINISTRATION

OPEN AIR AMPH. TO COMMONS DN.

OPEN AIR AMPH. TO COMMONS

OPEN AIR
AMPHITHEATER TO COMMONS

REC CENTER

STUDENT
RESOURCE
CENTER

CLASSROOMS

LABS

ATRIUM SPACE

SLOPE TO
EX. GRADES.

SECTION Nº 1

0 5 10'   30'

CLASSROOMS BEYOND

INTERIOR COMMONS   STUDENT
CENTER

SECTION Nº 2

0 5 10'   30'

CLASSROOMS BEYOND

ATRIUM SPACE
LABORATORIES BEYOND

OPEN AIR AMPHITHEATER

INTERIOR COMMONS OPEN AIR AMPHITHEATER

PARKING LEVEL
RAMP (PED) BEYOND.

94

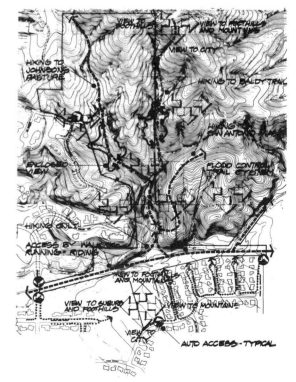

Index

aerial photograph   7
architecture   9
background   50, 46
base map   18
boats   54
branches   36, 38, 43
bubble diagram   17, 18
buildings   27, 28, 29, 59, 68
building style   27
car   54, 55
circular outline   35
closeup   72
conceptual diagram   15, 18
conceptual map   18
construction details   26, 59
continuous line   23
contour   23
contrast   53
curvilinear line   28
data map   14
decorative elements   54
depth   64, 76
design concept   11, 20
design education   6
design process   6
dimensioning   6, 17, 25, 29
dimension line   26
dotted line   22, 23
double line   28
elevation   9, 26, 59,
   60, 64, 66, 68, 76
evergreen   48
extralong dash   22

final site development plan   21
frontal plane   8, 60, 70
geometric form   28
grass   46
ground   31
ground cover   35, 44, 45, 46, 74
ground plane   32
height   31, 59
horizontal dimension   27, 59
landscape   59
landscape architecture   9
land use map   14
lettering guide   25
line   22, 44
line drawing   28
line width   25, 64
linework   22
long dash   22, 23
mass profile   25
master plan   21, 16
multiview projection   9
nonverbal communication   52
northern hemisphere   33
opacity   33
orthographic projection   7, 8, 60, 70
outline   36, 43
overlapping   38, 47
pavements   33, 50
people   54
perspective   64, 70
picture plane   8
plan   6, 9, 36, 41, 67
plan drawing
   7, 22, 32, 34, 46, 54, 59
plant materials
   27, 34, 35, 38, 68
preliminary design map   20, 40
profile line   26, 28
projection ray   8
regional map   13

road   56
roof form   29
scale   41
scaled model   11
scale indicator   54
section   6, 9, 59, 64, 66, 67, 68, 76
section drawing   22, 26
section—elevation   60
shading   30, 75
shadow   31, 32, 33, 76
shadow altitude   32
shadow angle   32
shadow bearing   32
short dash line   22, 23
shrubs   35, 41, 43, 48, 50, 74
site analysis map   19
site information map   14
soil map   14
space   34
spatial edges   34
sun   32, 75
sun side   30
supporting elements   68
surface condition   57
texture   26, 30, 33, 36, 38,
   43, 44, 45, 50, 74, 75
three-dimensional quality
   29, 31, 76
title block   25
tones   55
top view   9, 28
trees   35, 39, 43, 48
   70, 72, 73, 75
vegetation map   14
vertical dimension   59, 66
vertical exaggeration   66
vicinity map   13
viewer   6
water   52, 53
working drawing   25, 26
Zip-a-tone   64